It's All Me

The Modern Woman's Guide to Thriving After Divorce

VIVIAN HUGHES

Published and distributed in
the United States by Vivian Hughes, LLC,
www.vivhughes.com

Edited by Anrica Easley

Vivian Hughes, Principal
Vivian Hughes, LLC
PO Box 793411, Dallas, TX 75379
www.vivhughes.com
vivian@vivhughes.com

Library of Congress Cataloging-in-Publication Data

Hughes, Vivian
It's All Me, The Modern Woman's Guide to Thriving After Divorce
--1st Ed. & All Ed.

Print Edition ISBN 978-0-578-51685-1

Dedication

To our babies Lauren, Robert and Ryan:

We figured it out for you because you are worth it!
You were the reason we stopped our fighting
and learned to be family amicably.

We did it because "*that's what you do in a herd*!"
Quote from Diego in the movie Ice Age 2002

To every woman who feels as if she's losing her footing because of a broken heart, unrealized expectations, or just sheer disappointment, I want you to know I was there. Stuck in a dark place and feeling whole and happy was something I would never experience again, but I got out of my funk, and so can you.

I'm excited and humbled to share how I went from pissed off, let down, and hopeless to creating a dynamic co-parenting relationship with my ex-husband and experienced fun, fulfilling love again.

I'm hoping you'll read something in this book that inspires you to believe in yourself and the power of love again. Something that challenges you to rediscover your energy and make the small daily decisions that benefit you, your children, and your legacy.

You got this!

Vivian Hughes

Contents

Preface

Why did I write this book? For years people would ask me. "How in the hell do you get along so well with your ex-husband?" Women would stare at me with the most puzzling look on their faces, especially the women who knew my marriage history. They couldn't fathom how my ex and I could be 'family' after all we'd been through, and that's precisely why I wrote this book. To answer that question and to share not only *how* but *why*. Why did I want to include my ex on every call with our kid's teachers? How could I allow my ex into my home to help our kids organize their closets at the beginning of every school year and new year? Why would I share the license plate of guys that I dated with my ex-husband just in case things went to the left? Why not share that intel with my girlfriends and leave him out of it? After all, they are going to be the ones who have my back, not my ex. How could I love my ex's girlfriend from day one and grow to love her deeper as she became his fiancé? I admit it was crazy getting to a healthy place with him. The easiest part of our new dynamic was welcoming in the woman who would become our kids' bonus mom - I know she's in our lives because *I* manifested her (more on manifesting later).

The reality is, we all break up, and often it's bad blood in the mix. One or both people feel wronged and even hate each other. I hated my ex initially; for years!

But what about the children? What about our family's legacy? I figured out a few things that worked for me, and it's my prayer that it helps your family create a healthy flow as well. -Vivian Hughes

Introduction

*"…if the past cannot prevent you from being
present now, what power does it have?"*
- Eckhart Tolle, A New Earth

Yep, I married a man who clearly stated that he didn't want to be in a committed relationship at the onset of our dating, nor did he want to be married. Yep, I bought my wedding ring; I put it on my Service Merchandise credit card. This book is my story of taking full responsibility for my marriage and my divorce. Seeing my small children broken, feeling lost, and insecure pushed me to find a way to love their father after our divorce. Feeling their hurt forced me to decide to stop being a victim and start operating from a place of love. To heal me and to give my children space to be whole and secure.

Who am I? A girl from the east side of Detroit, Michigan. As a child, I knew there had to be something out there more than the ideas society fed me, but I fell into the trap of believing marriage was the be-all-end-all. Thinking I needed to be married to be a successful woman. I spent more time on education, work, and trying to fall in love and get married than I did on learning myself. Not learning myself as someone's daughter, student, or employee, but as a woman. I didn't take the time to ask myself: What do I like? What do I want? What makes me feel good? What do I want to experience, contribute, be, do, and have? NEVER did any of that come up for me to consider. It's like I was handed off from high school to college and from college to a job, and as a young working woman, my goal was to get married because, according to everything I saw, that is what happened next. The only thing I knew about marriage was what my church and societal influences taught me, and none of them taught me the importance of knowing myself and my worth first. I wasn't aware of the significance of knowing and honoring my body, my emotions, and my soul. I grew up in church and learned about the power of God, but He was out there and not in me, so I didn't internalize my connection with God.

I was over 40 years old when I learned I could use my word as my wand and speak things over my life that would manifest. That's the piece I learned after I lost my home to foreclosure and my car to repossession. After moving from Detroit to Dallas with no money, no job, and only a sliver of hope is when I learned this. I learned this after my marriage of 13 years ended in divorce. These are the pieces I'm sharing with you throughout the pages of this book. So, don't skip ahead; keep reading one page at a time because I promise you there is value on every page of this book.

-Vivian Hughes

One

The Magic Of Intention

What do you want?
What do you believe you can have?

Y ou have the power! The power to shift every relationship in
your life. The ability to decide how you want your life to look
and the power to manifest those desires regularly. Without
understanding your capabilities and how to direct them, you cannot
fully step into command and create your life. You'll be frustrated
with your ex, your children will see it, and you'll feel bad that you're
in this tumultuous relationship. You'll wonder, "why me?" You'll
regret the decision you made to marry him or criticize him and try
to beat him into seeing the error of his ways verbally. You'll cry in
secret, pray faithfully for a breakthrough, and try to put on a good
face for your children. You'll see other people who seemingly have it
together and wonder, "What do they know that I don't?" You'll find
a tribe of hurt baby mommas to commiserate with and dig yourself
deeper into a sadness that is only comforted by knowing others are
just as miserable as you are. And this cycle can last forever. I know
women who started as bitter mothers and matured into bitter
grandmothers. It takes effort and commitment to go through the
process of healing this line of thinking and living. Our mindsets
don't generally auto-correct, but once you tap into it, I promise you,
you'll be glad you did.

When I began learning about my powers in my early 40's, I was pissed that no one told me this when I was younger. How could my mom, grandma, aunts, and family elders not know this information, and if they did, why didn't they share it with me and my generation? I quickly reconciled my feelings when I realized my elders were growing up at a different time, and they didn't know this information. They didn't have the internet. They didn't have YouTube to binge-watch personal development videos.

Through this book, be prepared to be reminded of what you knew before society seduced your powers away from you. I share with you the exact steps to access your capacity, and through the application of the information I share with you in this book, you will experience a perspective shift. I ask that you keep an open mind.

Now, before we dive in, let's do a quick exercise for resonance. Close your eyes and take three deep breaths. Then, silently or aloud, ask yourself, "What is my intention? What am I seeking to learn from this book? Who do I want to be after I read this book? What will my family's theme be after I read this book?" Now, write down everything that comes to your mind. Don't question it. Just write it, whatever comes up. Take as long as you need for this exercise because it may be the most valuable exercise you complete. You might finish this exercise in three minutes, or it could take you three hours or even three days to flush out your truths. I'm asking you right now, with every fiber of my being, please do not skip this step. Take all the time you need because setting your intention is the equivalent of entering an address into your GPS. And we all know, regardless of the reroutes, you'll reach your planned destination as long as you maintain your intention. Maybe you'll read something that causes you to dream about a scenario that sparks your 'ah-ha' moment. Or perhaps the clarity you seek will come to you while you're in the shower days after you read passages of this book. Whatever, however, whenever, this is YOUR journey, and by setting your intention, you've partnered with God, Source, The Divine, Love and Light, Creator, your ancestors, your spirit guides, your higher self, whomever you connect with as your Source and support. therefore, YOU SHALL RECEIVE! #praisebreak

The overarching goal for reading this book is to learn how to navigate and recover from disappointment, heartbreak, and divorce with peace and optimism. I am living proof that a *proper* release from a discordant marriage can translate into a golden era for you and your family. Even if things are distressing at the moment, you can turn it around. It will take some work but consider the most important thing:

> What if your divorce can transform & elevate you,
> your ex, and your children if repurposed?

There are ways to create beauty out of ugly. We all know dirt and manure are great fertilizers used to grow flowers, so the filthy mess of your divorce or the breaking up with your child's father may be the perfect foundation to cultivate your best life, but it's up to you to decide.

Housekeeping: To gain the maximum benefit from this book, let's agree that we are a global family of sisters. When we put our hearts together, we will heal our families, communities, and even the planet. But our energy has to flow toward progress rather than mere survival. Also, let's agree that as the woman heals, she heals the man and the community, not by doing anything to him, but by how she shows up. As she recovers, the essence of who she is, her energy, her posture, and her words awaken the king in him. Many of us focus our energy on putting on a brave smile for the kids, hiding our mortally wounded and broken hearts. I was all too good at convincing friends and family that I had everything under control and that I was ok, but I was far from ok.

I believe as we bring our hearts and minds into a harmonious space, our bodies will relax and stop producing stress hormones, and as we come out of fight or flight mode and into harmony, our bodies will suffer less from dis-ease.

The golden era of our lives requires
a level of self-mastery that needs training and support.
This book is a manual to that end.

Real talk? Healing from divorce will likely be the *most* challenging thing you've ever done, but it can also be the most eye opening as your gateway into self-mastery!

Many women are merely enduring a divorce, barely dealing with the feeling of loss and betrayal that inherently comes with the process. I know, all too well, that dissolving a marriage can be comparable to a brutal boxing match. And at its worse, divorce can be likened to one of those *underground* fight clubs, with no-moves-barred and blood splatter on the walls. But while you bob and weave, staying clear of the knock-out punch, there's something more you can do to win the title.

Even if relationships have devolved into a contentious series of chaos, there is a way to not only survive the process but to thrive! What if wisdom is the only thing standing between you and the life you've always intended? What if it isn't a matter of luck, beauty, or having lots of money? What if living your best life is more comfortable than living the life for which you've settled?

Success stories pop up worldwide; information, and testimonies that offer creative tools for cultivating an amicable separation, uncoupling, and divorce.

For many, the first step is merely believing in the possibility of transformation for you and your family. Second is the need for mastery of the tools and modalities that activate the change.

Let's kick-start things with a quick release exercise:

EXERCISE 1.1

Release & Surrender Letters
(DO NOT GIVE THESE LETTERS AWAY– THESE ARE FOR YOU TO KEEP AND/OR BURN)

Are you holding a grudge against your ex? Are you blaming him for how your life is today? Do you feel as if your experience would've been better if you or he would've been different?

Today, put it all on paper. Grab a few sheets of paper and write out what you're pissed about, and at the end, write, "I surrender my hurt, pain, disappointment, anger, and resentment, and I go free to live a life of love, peace, harmony, and joy." You can keep this letter in your prayer box, journal, or you can burn it.

> *CAUTION: be safe when burning paper; it can blow and ignite other items. I go in my back yard and burn letters in the barbeque grill or an old pot; I never burn paper in the house.*

If you're able to go to the next step of this process, also write, "I forgive you (insert name here) for any and every reason that I've held contempt in my heart towards you. I bless you, and I release you to your greatest good."

Now I know the forgiveness letter might be a bit of a challenge initially, and it's ok if you decide to skip it for now. Keep moving forward in the book, just flag the page as something to revisit later. If you're reading this book, I believe you'll return to the forgiveness exercise in time.

Remember: Don't give the letter to the person; this isn't about them. It's about you, shred it or burn it, and visualize yourself free from the burden of harboring unforgiveness.

Loss of Covering

I recall, from many years ago, the anxiety of my then-pending divorce. I wondered how I would ensure my children were safe and able to flourish despite my divorce. How would I? I laid awake at night, imagining ways to replace him in our household. I thought if I could meet the right guy, we'd still have the male presence in the house. Yes, the kids would have routine time with their dad, but how would I fill the void of the now-absent male energy?

I felt the loss of a covering. While the marriage didn't work, being married offered some solace. I had the comfort of having a man physically in the house. It's incredible how the presence of a man in the house held reassurances – even when that man was, arguably, a source of pain and emotional peril.

Once you've been a wife, you may develop a dependency on having that role. It's not uncommon for women to date less than our worth in exchange for having a man's presence and for the feeling of belonging to someone. It's pretty safe to assume if you haven't healed from the divorce, there's some active pain attracting men who know they don't have to show up for you because you're wounded. These men can smell blood in the dating waters and realize you aren't clear on what you deserve, that you will compromise some of your standards, and you will allow the unallowable just so that you aren't alone.

My ex-husband and I were inseparable at one point. It was us-against-the-world, and a part of me felt we were better than divorce. I felt let-down, dishonored, and discarded. I invested in numerous business ideas and properties to support my ex's hopes and dreams.

Yes, I knew we were a power couple. We had creative ideas, a local following, and revenue-generating businesses. He was 32 years old, had swag, a healthy business, and connections. I was a gorgeous 24-year-old who was brilliant, had the business savvy, a great job in management for Chrysler Corporation, and an ever-growing savings account. We had all the ingredients needed to live that power-couple lifestyle, and we did, but it was short-lived, and after our 12th anniversary, something in me knew it was over.

While married, he and I threw well-attended parties together in Detroit at the Detroit West Club. We hired our family as the caterer, family for security, family to collect tickets, and family to take photos. The family was everything to us. I remember the feeling of walking through a crowd of guests on his arm with immense pride. I'm slaying corporate; our hair salon was always packed, and we hosted the one party that anyone who knew us dropped what they had planned to be in attendance. I can see it now as I revisit the scene in my head to get it on these pages for you. It was spectacular! Oh, and the way he'd hug me as we greeted guests or pose for pictures was all the reassurance I needed. Never in a million years would I ever think we'd get a divorce. We shared eleven years of holidays and birthdays. We put out fires and solved problems with one another. We made love and fell asleep watching movies together. The loving energy of those moments still lurked in my distant memory. Despite the arguments and drama, there was a part of me that needed to mourn the loss of the good things that we shared. The bad didn't negate the good, and it took me years to realize that and to adjust. To adjust to seeing the last decade as a blessing. We built and shared experiences that would survive the divorce—many of which we will carry for the rest of our lives.

I mourned that our marriage failed
& I wondered how the hell was
I going to do life alone!

Husbands provide wives unique energy that can't be substituted, and when it's gone, though you may feel he doesn't deserve you anymore and even pretend to be completely relieved, there's a measured loss. It's similar to when a bulb goes out in a chandelier. The chandelier is still beautiful and functional, but you can see that it lost a little something. The family is your chandelier; figuring out how to restore the missing bulb to bring it back to its full radiance is the work.

Was it My Fault?

On the days that I took a break from mourning what could have been, I wondered what I should have done.

> I tortured myself rehashing past scenarios
> with my ex, berating myself for not saying this
> or doing that – and dancing around the
> idea that the divorce was *somehow* my fault.

I began to snap out of that funk when I came to grips with the fact that out of all the men I knew, I *chose* to marry my ex-husband. I realized my decision would have to be owned and reconciled on some level.

Thus, admitting culpability in the situation freed me. I could face facts and learn my lessons. Putting on my big-girl panties helped me own the part of things that came by my consent, my blindness, apathy, denial, unfinished childhood issues, and my willingness to give away my power and compromise my standards. #settle

Here's the hard pill to swallow: some part of my marital failure is my fault if only to admit that he was my choice out of all the other men on the planet. Divorce is a two-way street, so women's tendency to fervently argue complete innocence in hopes of gaining some relationship reprieve or community support is impractical, deceitful, and impotent.

I can only learn from the mistakes that I claim as my own, not the ones I deny.

Have I Ruined My Life?

There's a hassling sentiment that plays in some women's heads: being a single mom will guarantee a lonely life. After all, who wants to help raise another man's children? Where are the eligible bachelors who are signing up to deal with and tolerate a spirited ex-husband? Who wants all this baggage? These questions encouraged my cruel tendency to punish myself. They also serve as some of the motives behind why women stay too long in particular relationships.

The reasons we stay in toxic relationships are the same reasons that we wallow in self-pity.

I once heard a popular female evangelist share that her husband had prayed for an opportunity to marry a woman who needed his help. He had grown up in a loving home, and he knew some people had quite the opposite start in life. As a bachelor, he desired marriage with a woman who needed him to heal and learn how to trust again. He wanted to serve as a husband but in a particular and unique way. He didn't have a desire for a wife in the traditional sense. He prayed to God for an aggrieved woman, to be the vessel through which her restoration flowed. This story reminds me of Ne-Yo's song lyrics; let me love you until you learn to love yourself.

Sometimes, what a woman sees as her ruin is a *certain* man's opportunity and place of fulfillment.

One night after listening to me complain and wallow in self-pity, one of my dearest friends told me, "Girl, you heard Kanye's lyrics in Gold Digger? He said the woman he went out with has four kids, and he was taking them and their friends to Showbiz in a Benz. So quit tripping and making up a worst-case scenario. Plenty of men will sign up for your baggage." Then we laughed as we talked about other friends who had kids and a healthy relationship with good men. That conversation was the beginning of me viewing my situation completely different. I no longer had a mindset of lack relating to myself or what was available to me. My package wasn't insufficient or burdensome.

> *Note: Keep you a friend around like that one! If you don't have one, pray and ask for one to flow into your life, and you'll get one!*

My package was abundant; my family was a blessing! Juggling kids between practices, recitals, doctor's appointments, after-school activities, and sports wasn't a burden; it was a blessing, and what better place to pour energy into, to sow? Once that became my mindset, I attracted men who were very ready to be a stepdaddy – great men, who I appreciated, loved, and respected but not as my life partner. I wanted to take my time, learn about my power, and fall in love with myself for the first time.

I had options, and they were bountiful – to think, it all started with a shift in my perspective, and voila, I attracted the very men who reflected me, how I felt about myself and my family. This energy worked wonders as it related to how I felt about my ex. He was no longer my source; I realized everything I needed was within me. I created my solutions from the essence of my being. Whether that be a job, promotion, money, a date, friends, supporters, it all emitted from the core of my being and attracted the same to me. Subsequently, anything my ex did or didn't do was his choice. I saw his contribution as his seed to sow in his garden of life – I made requests and told him what needed to happen, but that was it. I didn't feel called to hold him accountable because I realized it was his opportunity to sow and his choice.

*   **FULL DISCLOSURE: THIS DID NOT HAPPEN OVERNIGHT NOR WAS IT A ONE AND DONE MINDSET SHIFT. ***

I would get enraged, and no matter how much I tried, there was a button that my ex could push, and it would piss me exhaustively off. None more than when he would text me and say he was going out of town, and I'd have to pick up the kids. This was not our arrangement and would require me to leave work at a peak time for my team. However, after growing tired of being reactive, I tapped into my Divine Goddess toolbox and decided to communicate with his girlfriend. This reach out was not to be messy; this was to get everybody on the same page. It was 'Operation Take Care of the Kids First,' so I decided to send a group text. I explained the hardship and gave her full visibility because I don't know what impression my ex gave his girlfriend. I believed she'd help develop an amicable solution because she was terrific, and remember, I manifested her into his/ our lives. Voila, she did! They coordinated with their friends who the children knew and loved and arranged for them to be picked up, fed, and dropped off at home. PERFECT! Yes, my Divine Goddess energy manifested a peaceful solution, and so will yours.

Are you familiar with how energy and desire work? Or how about the works of Wayne Dyer? If not, make a note right now to search for Wayne Dyer on YouTube and binge watch him. I'll also include some of my favorite Wayne Dyer videos on the It's All Me site. In a nutshell, your desire for a partner with a specific set of tolerances means that he already exists. You're aligning with him through your willingness to experience him. What appears to be challenging or burdensome to you is a calling for love to heal yourself and a blessing to him.

Everything you will ever need in life already exists. It's prepared and waiting for you to ask, believe, and receive when it presents itself to you.

However, the thing that determines whether you will allow a loving man into your life is your ability to trust that he exists before you meet him and your ability to accept him into your life when he shows up. More on that later!

Any misguided decisions you've made out of lack of knowledge, jaded perspective, or sheer desperation to stay too long and tolerate certain behaviors, does not warrant a life sentence of lonely regret.

One of the worse things you can do to your kids is to let them see you give up on yourself. Our children understand how they are to perceive the world by watching us. Showing them how you process grief and bounce back helps them know shit happens, but resilience is in their DNA. It was difficult for me to get out of the fetal position for years, but when I discovered the powerful insight that I'm sharing with you in this book, my entire life changed. So beautiful, dynamic, equipped woman, I have a question for you. Would you concede to living in darkness when you have access to the light switch? My soul desires that you find your light switch in these pages for yourself and your legacy. Our children learn models of grace under fire, resilience, courage, forgiveness, and self-love lessons and restoration by watching us.

We know our kids are watching and taking notes, and our mistakes won't break them, but our refusal to *learn* from our mistakes will subject them to trying to make sense out of non-sense.

Be assured that you are worthy of a dynamic relationship with a man – one that is the total package. But it starts with you seeing yourself as the complete package. We don't attract what we want in the future; we attract who we are in the moment. As you read this book, you'll begin to see yourself and your package as the blessing it is. You'll honor your desire for a partner from a space of worthiness and expectancy. You are not needy or desperate; you are not lucky to find a good man. As you heal and get clear on what you deserve and desire, men will come out of seemingly nowhere. Go about your business and watch how many delightful suitors you meet along your journey.

Also, know, there is a way for your children to grow healthy & well-adjusted without being broken by divorce.

Betrayal and No Accountability

Being betrayed by the man with whom I co-created life was earth-shattering. I thought my gifts meant something – my womb, my birth, and care for our children. I felt it earned me a place of respect.

I thought *my* fidelity would inspire and maintain *his* loyalty. And when this didn't prove to be the case, I thought I'd get more support from family members to help "get him in line."

Neglected, unfairly scorned, and fully expected to get over everything on my own, I felt alone. No matter how supportive our families were during our union, a clear line was drawn in the sand when the marriage was over. Some of my coaching clients are surprised to find that their husbands' families often support their husbands' behavior regardless of the depravity. The adage blood is thicker than water when used to divide is ignorant. The children are the blood, so their legacy benefits from being united, not picking sides against the dueling parents. It's frustrating to see family members directing their energy in divisive ways instead of rallying around to help the feuding stop. I appreciated my ex's aunt and uncle giving him wise counsel when I acted selfishly and foolishly out of pain. He shared with me they told him his position in his children's lives is all that matters, and as a part of that, he needed to be present regularly whether we are together or not. And to always work towards keeping the peace and working together even if he had to lead that charge. They gave him marching orders to be the best ex-husband ever. I remember thinking if we had a community of elders who would confront and correct husbands that miss the bar, maybe the incidents would be fewer. Accountability to the elders, the village, and the family's economic base would cause the man to pause and consider the impact of his actions on a grander scale.

It's true, a community and tribe that supports family and condemns infidelity would be a welcomed help. I have a friend who worked for an orthodox religious community. She shared how she witnessed them vigorously condemned adultery as a group. The other men were ashamed of the offending husband. They saw him as pathetic – a man without charge over his faculties. The cheating man was dealt with as if he were a weak link, someone that posed a threat to their way of life, and they quickly rallied to ensure he remedied whatever issues that contributed to his marital failure.

I would think in *that* environment - a woman is not left alone to fight the battle. There can be reconciliation with clear boundaries and an apparent rebuke for the offending behavior. That supportive environment would make divorce a last result because the community provided proper accountability. I am amazed that different cultures have such a contrast in reaction to identical conduct on the same planet.

In any event, we have recourse – with or without the support of others. The first step is to understand that our Source is not our husband, family, or friends.

People are the vessel, but they are not our Source!

If a man decides to maintain his role as a leader, provider, and protector of his family, he uses his power to enable the Source to flow through him as a vessel. However, suppose he chooses to use his control for his selfish delight, neglecting his family. In that case, he misses the opportunity to sow into the garden that is his family, but the family still flourishes. Man is not the Source of love, protection, provision, stability; he's the vessel. Remember, Source will flow through another willing and receptive vessel, so there is no family loss. It's a loss to the man who opted out of being the vessel. God, Source, Creator will always be able to bypass him and provide for the family by a litany of other methods.

God has infinite contingencies. The man will miss his opportunity to sow into the garden that is his children, but this does not relegate the children to living a life of lack.

God, Source, Higher Power, whatever you call this Infinite Intelligence, can bypass him and provide for the family by a litany of other channels.

The Source/vessel concept is real regarding friends, family, government, religious organizations – and every other channel in your life; they are all replaceable because they are not your Source. Once you set your intention, the provisions will manifest.

While there may be a need for counseling and therapies as you decide on divorce, you must tend to your self-care and refuse any "scarlet letter" of shame or regret once you make your choice.

Yes, learn your lessons and own your part, but by all means, take steps to process the feelings and make your peace with divorce.

Mindset Reset: Shift & Create

Mindset work saved me from a life of perpetual imbalance. It's something so simple to do, and we all can do it, but many of us don't know how to do it because we haven't learned. Before I speak to anyone in the morning, I talk to myself. I open my mouth and say something like this 'Today, I am open and receptive to more love, joy, and opportunities than I've ever experienced or imagined. Today, I am on purpose, and everything I think, say, and do aid me in living a truly fulfilled life. Today I am full of creative ideas, and I am a walking, breathing magnet. Everything I encounter Today is working for my greatest good, be it wanted or unwanted. Today, I release all resentment. I forgive myself and everyone else because hey, we're all trying to figure this thing out, so I'm not judging or taking anything personally. I release myself from any judgment, and I'm proud of who I am right now, as-is. I am valuable, worthy, whole, and complete.

I got this, let's do this!' Whew, I felt that as I wrote it here for you! After that powerful self-talk, I do a 15-minute meditation, turn on some morning music and flow through my grooming, wake the kids up, grab a bite for breakfast, and then get to work! In essence, I start every day as a new woman with a fresh intention and a new level of belief. Have you ever seen a coach give a locker room pep talk to his team right before a game? The entire purpose of this talk is to remind the players of who they are, what they are expected to accomplish on the field or court, and mentally and energetically make them own the feeling of victory before putting one foot on the field or court. We rise early in the morning and dedicate time to mindset work, writing meditations, exercise, affirmations, forgiveness journals, etc. to allow ourselves time and space to clear the ideas and expectations that bind us. Mindset work uncovers the illusory expectations that we assumed were realistic. Mindset work pivots us into a life of intention and prevents us from reacting and moving through our day on autopilot. Every day being similar to the one before it, and none seeming to bring with it the breath of fresh air we long to feel.

Trying to do too much to be a superwoman is the fastest way to fail at self-care.

Women deserve to give themselves permission to ask for and require assistance. I know of too many women who can afford housekeeping services but refuse to hire help because of some overbearing standard of domestic excellence. This antiquated belief system is the folly of ego masquerading as discipline, and it is the chief reason many women may never build their dream and empire. They could be making calls or writing blogs for their business instead of spending time scratching off toothpaste splatter from the mirror in the bathroom.

Ladies, your emotional well-being, your health and fulfillment in life is in your purpose. Ask yourself if it's time to let go of some of that purpose snatching programming whereby a woman proves her worth by cleaning her house and running her errands. A housekeeper and an assistant are not a luxury in 2020; they are borderline essential. One of my clients, a C level executive, shared with me how she vacillated over hiring help – because the thought is that "I should be able to do all of this." It's crazy how we, women, have been conditioned to believe we should be able to do it all. Not only absurd, but it's also unhealthy, and in many cases, our bodies are giving us signals that it's in overload mode.

We need support to live well on the planet as women, mothers, daughters, ex-wives, teachers, evangelists, mechanics, cooks, entrepreneurs, etc. Mindset work renews our mind and trains us to recalibrate our guidelines and the expectation for our lives. It permits us to ask for deliverance.

The inability to receive quality support and assistance is a sneaky form of self-abuse because it is impossible to be independent.

I don't see how it's humanly possible for anyone to make 6 or 7 figures independent of mentors, platforms, books, lawyers, tax accountants, advocates, personal assistants, etc. We all need and deserve support and help to win in life. Pray for and look for your team of supporters and accept their assistance with dignity.

Be on the lookout for the feeling that you are a burden or that requesting support to help care for your children is a hard ask, that it's *your* assignment to manage solely, and if you need help, you're 'not a good mom.'

That mentality makes your focus more on finding ways to avoid needing resources rather than finding ways to let resources flow.

That mindset creates a dread of asking and makes it feel uncomfortable. I know being in the vulnerable position of needing an ex-husband to show up for the kids, especially in a way that makes *your* life easier, may promote a needling frustration and anger when he doesn't cooperate. So much so that a human moment of wrath, complete with fire and brimstone, may be warranted on occasion. But once you express the anger, course correct back toward forgiveness and grace. Be pissed at the moment, but don't stay pissed off. Holding bitterness looks ugly on a face and what we focus on we attract, so let it go as soon as possible.

If for the last ten years, you've been mad at your ex-husband for what he did and you're having a hard time shaking the bitterness, consider that the lines in your face tell it. You wear unexpressed anger in and on your body. It's less likely that you'll attract better opportunities or more evolved companions with old energy tethered by anger for your ex and fear of getting help from others.

If you do your mindset reset work, your word will become your wand, as Florence Scovel Shinn writes in her book, *The Game of Life and How to Play It*. As you grow financially – and you will, you'll no longer nervously wait for your ex-husband's responses or regular support payments (that's if you don't have a court order in place). Remember, always be willing to receive his contribution as he grows as a person, and that's for his sake. It is beneficial for him to provide and do his part as a parent and adult. Nevertheless, keep your effort and energy pointed to your real Source and refuse the frustrating position of waiting on him.

I want you to let seep into your mind that your ex-husband is not your Source; he is a vessel. If your children's Dad is absentee, the children will miss him and long for him, but have faith that no good thing will be withheld from you or your kids. Align your focus and energy on what you desire for your family - and step into that feeling. As you operate from that space, you'll feel inspired to take specific actions that position you for opportunities that seem miraculous, out of the blue, even serendipitous regularly. Remember, you're the creator of your reality or the victim of your existence; you can't be both.

Again, your Source is God, Infinite Intelligence, Divine Source Energy, or whatever you prefer to call it, be it Heavenly Father or Elizabeth – the energy will manifest that which is a match. It's never destroyed, absent or withholding.

State your request, provide the supporting factors, flush out the details during the conversation, and then hush.

Remember, whatever your ex does is sowing seed in his garden of life; you and your children won't lack. Your focus is on building your trust and relationship with God and believing your desires are already met through infinite intelligence.

Let your prayer and affirmation be that your children are always surrounded by the proper people and conditions that encourage their inner splendor to come forth.

Even if your ex sabotages things and refuses to sufficiently help the children, resist the temptation to be bitter and vindictive. Your reaction to this behavior could spoil the sweetness that is your Divine nectar and jack up your attraction and flow with your new opportunities. It isn't easy, but it's worth it – please believe me. Understand, if your ex-husband senses you depend on him and that he can insight a reaction from you, he may resist all the more in a mean-spirited attempt to have an impact on you, good or bad; sometimes ex's don't care, just getting your attention is a W for them. Now that's not all men, some are upright, high vibrational, and protective of their legacy. The battle of the exes is, unfortunately, typical. I'm in several divorce groups on social media, and I see the low-down dirty tactics some men use to get attention or prove a point. You heard our former First Lady Michelle Obama say it best, "when they go low, we go high" well, she wasn't talking about ex-husbands in that speech; however, it certainly applies here. You let him go low, and you take the high ground.

That's *his* karma!

Don't be bitter and shut him out because that will likely backfire at some point, making you out to be the rabble-rouser. Not to mention you can't sink to the level of fighting and remain at a high vibration energetically, so you're turning off your radiance and magnetism, which delays the miracles and manifestations you're creating. You're too consciously aware of who you are, so don't stoop to playing tit-for-tat; that's beneath you Divine Goddess and besides, being in that low energy space is a sure way to delay the process of healing yourself and your family.

Know that Source will send other vessels, fulfilling every need for you and your family; delight in that! Instead of getting riled up for an epic rap battle with your ex – take a deep breath, smile and with gratitude count your blessings and then breathe in what you've envisioned for your family and say thank you as you hold that image in your mind. Do not be concerned with how things will manifest, focus on believing, and be courageous enough to launch into inspired action when you get the nudge. Remain gracious and receive provisions as they display.

I remember receiving multiple raises and job offers after calming down all the crazy energy during and after my divorce. One employer nearly doubled my income, and then another one increased my salary by 25%. Understand none of that happened when I was bitter, vengeful, and low vibrational. There's no sustainable benefit in being a victim or vindictive. Yes, being a victim gets you an audience, but it doesn't bring you the healing you desire and deserve. You lessen your chances of being whole and attracting dates with dynamic, loyal, family men by playing a victim, but the bloodhounds will gladly listen to you bash your ex. They listen as you tell them the same move they need to make to get what they want from you. But this is nothing you have to worry about when you're whole. You'll intuitively know how to identify when a bloodhound is approaching you, and the essence of who you are, coupled with your honey-laced, laser-sharp words, will politely send him back to the lower vibration camp. I learned this the hard way. Every area of my life suffered, and as I tried to date to fill the void, I dated the bloodhounds.

During the most stressful points of my divorce, my hair fell out, I had the worse acne ever, and my bank account went negative month after month.

Things didn't begin to lift until I faced the fact that I had walked down the church aisle and married the man. I had to admit that I chose to purchase the home and decided to have the kids, so I didn't get to play the little victim. As I owned my part, I began to see the correlation between my mindset and my credit score.

I realized that if I was going to be a victim,
everything was going to victimize me.
Life would rob me, tax me, and overcharge me
because that matched the energy and
mindset I harbored.

I noticed that how I did one thing was how I did everything. I didn't have certain areas in my life that saw me as a consistent warrior and victor and others that saw me as a wimp. The beliefs I had about myself in my marriage and divorce was what I thought about myself at work or while pulling into a crappy parking space at the supermarket. When I felt like a victim in one thing, I tended to lean into being a victim in everything else.

I recall looking at a photo of a younger me with my sorority sisters. I had plans and goals, but I had lost that version of myself in the labyrinth of victimhood, blaming, and martyrdom. However, as

I elevated my self-esteem by faithfully doing mindset exercises to redirect my thought patterns, every part of my life lifted. My conversations with my ex-husband became more fluid and livelier, and over time, I began to attract viable suiters, eligible men who were eager to be not only a part of my life but a part of my family's too. Circumstances seemed to come together magically, and it was all because I flipped the script and learned how to forgive my ex. And most importantly, I learned how to forgive and feel good about myself. I felt worthy of the right to ask for what I needed from Source boldly and expect it to become a part of my life.

EXERCISE 1.2

What does someone get when they get you?

In this exercise, you focus on you. All things YOU!

Are you a fantastic cook? Can you host large family gatherings? Do you have a soothing energy that heals and calms those around you? What do people compliment you on? Are you a fabulous assistant, lawyer, organizer, teacher, cook, doctor, strategist, communicator, speaker, housekeeper, engineer, musician, photographer, etc.?

Action: List 21 traits that describe what you bring to the table, and don't be modest here - toot your own horn!

In the space below, list your talents, skills, and abilities.

If you get stuck, ask your close friends to tell you how you add value to their life? What are your strengths?

This exercise is a critical step, so don't skip it.

Mindset Mastery Exercise

Ex: Great w/Excel	Invigorating energy	Nurturing

Two
How Did I Get Here?

"When you come out of the storm, you won't be
the same person who walked in.
That's what this
storm's all about."
— Haruki Murakami

P lease take a bold look at the choices that led to this place – the dark territory of divorce. For me, the introspection made me take an authentic look at the way everything transpired.

While I want to believe I did everything right,
the truth is, I had something to do with it all,
including the things that went wrong.

From day one, my ex-husband told me that he never wanted to be in a committed, monogamous relationship. That should have stopped me cold.

Instead, about a year later, I took him to Service Merchandise, picked out my wedding ring, put it on my credit card, and my mother called the church office to get our ceremony on the calendar before the end of 1997. I pulled my ex into my fantasy and expected him to know his lines and play the role. While he didn't refuse to go along with our delusional marriage, he *did* leave a trail of crumbs that would have led to the truth had I cared to find it. After acknowledging I swept multiple crumbs of truth under our marital rug, I couldn't honestly say that divorce was a big surprise. I bet most women reading this book can admit to the same dynamic concerning their divorce.

I've informally surveyed women complaining about their husbands, and they often admit that they married the potential. They confessed that the man had many red flags when they married him, and they were hoping to fix him on the go. Most of them admit their husbands were consistent with the red flags, but they held hope that he'd grow into the relationship and give in to it eventually.

Now, this will take a little faith on your part but believe me when I tell you that owning your choice has medicine and magic in it.

When you release the victim moniker, you position yourself to forgive your own choices, which is the best rehearsal for finally forgiving others. Being free and clear of vengeance or vendettas enables you to learn the golden lesson that hardship taught you. Lastly, mastering those life lessons positions you for wiser choices and better outcomes, presently and in your glorious future.

Realize being able to create a mess inherently means you are also able to develop a solution. Again, being a creator is good news because creating an experience of any kind, divorce or otherwise, is proof you're able to conceive overall. You are a walking powerhouse of faith, expectation, hope, and imagination, and when you wield those powers more skillfully, you'll get more of what you truly desire. But be warned, this creative force requires a disciplined restraint from blaming others, including blaming yourself.

Acknowledging our mistakes to learn a lesson is lightyears away from blaming ourselves.

Blaming yourself creates a feeling that you don't deserve a break or a breakthrough. Blame holds the dark clouds of life over your head, blocking blessings. It is a root of the doom and gloom energy that so many of us carry. Blame is like saying you should've, or I should've. Contemplating what should be is denying the present reality, and that's delusional because the only thing that's real is now the current reality. "Should" is not an encouraging word; it is a word that implies lack. Eliminate it from your vocabulary as it relates to your life. Shift the should've talk to I am, I feel, I have talk. For instance, I should've known better shifts to, now that I know better, I am positioned to do better. Or I should've done something different changes to; now that I have new insights, I have a different perspective and can make different choices. I also believe should is a cop-out. I often hear women go on and on about what they would do differently in their past if they would've known then what they know now. Going backward in your mind doesn't change what happened. When I hear people go back in thought, I often ask them to project out twenty years from now and tell me what yourself twenty years from now would say. Then I ask them to focus on carrying that vision out. Looking back brings up feelings of regret. There's no magic adjustment in the timeline of your life but try your hand at projecting and creating; you may find that to be a sweet spot.

EXERCISE 1.3

Action: Sit in a quiet space. Play a miracle meditation tone softly (there are plenty to choose from on YouTube)

Take 3 deep cleansing breaths.

Now envision yourself in 20 years. For example, if you're 42, imagine yourself at 62. What words of wisdom does your future-self give your present-day self?

Take some time and breathe through this. Close your eyes as you ask the question and begin to witness your thoughts become more evident. Write what comes up.

Think about your health and wellness, family life, love life, financial life, and career life. Whatever comes up. Envision yourself as the elder of the village imparting wisdom that's seemingly channeled or downloaded from God.

Don't skip this step.

_____

_____

_____

_____

_____

_____

_____

_____

Mindset
Mastery
Exercise

Consider this, creating desirable outcomes requires intention. There is an attractiveness to a woman who is queen-like. Who forgives because she understands people are doing the best they can, and their behavior isn't about her. Instead, it's them projecting and deflecting as they deal with their triggers and traumas. A woman who takes the position of needing nothing, being everything, and having access to what she needs when she needs it because she knows she IS IT. Granted, developing this mindset is a nuanced process. It requires a spiritual sophistication but refusing the habit of blaming yourself and him for past mistakes can be a breakthrough method of getting faith and creative power active in your life.

Walking in constant grace and mercy toward yourself and others requires an understanding that people are doing the best they can. When things are low vibrational or negative, that likely means they are operating out of a lacking mindset and broken nature. Sometimes grace is the healing balm that inspires a person's growth exponentially. When my ex-husband realized I no longer blamed him for our outcomes, I noticed a profound, physical change in his countenance.

My Ex-husband was waiting to be let off the hook as the bad guy that ruined everything.

I soon realized that some of the post-divorce behavior and resistance I got from him were born out of frustration with my lack of *true* forgiveness. But when I admitted that he tried to communicate with me, he wanted me to be his girlfriend exclusively before our marriage while he continued to date other women. My acknowledgment that my ex-husband shared upfront, he was not entirely sold on getting married but had resigned himself to it to avoid violating the standard of conduct set by my mother and me.

When he failed to follow-through with behavior becoming a "good husband," it was unfair to make him the only problem in the scenario.

I had my agenda when we married. I ignored the signs my ex gave me, stayed too long when things went south, manipulated, and covered-up so much that I was equally guilty of co-creating a mess of a marriage. I was determined to make this thing work, and I wanted what I wanted. I had decided that the only way to get the white picket fence was to make concessions and strong-arm my way into that life. That arrogance facilitated a doomed marriage and a contentious divorce. But soon, I realized that we didn't have to walk that out for the rest of our lives.

My decision to admit my part in the divorce, grant forgiveness for us both & count both him and me blameless changed both our lives.

My life and love expanded when I refrained from campaigning as a martyr and when I owned my delusional manipulations. I redefined my values and scrutinized my upbringing and a matrix of other influences.

When I decided that I was worthy of forgiveness and blamelessness, I organically transitioned into someone who needed to give that gift to others.

I began to master forgiveness, holding all parties blameless, and I came out the other side, reclaiming my power and feminine divinity.

What's more Divine than granting absolution? You're offering forgiveness to benefit yourself. This exoneration is setting you free to live your best life truly. The other person doesn't have to deserve it, earn it, or even receive it; you just have to give it. Once you forgive, that monkey is off your back. The hands you use to hold him hostage become free when you release your grip. This freedom allows you to create and receive. Take a second right now to hold something; anything. Your cell phone a cup, or better yet, just hold your other hand. Right now, your hands are clasped together. If I threw a ball at you, you wouldn't be able to catch it without letting go. If I tried to put a one-hundred-dollar bill in your hands, you wouldn't be able to receive it because you're holding something already. Does this make sense? Holding anyone hostage makes you the warden; at the end of the day, you're both in jail.

So, release! You are lighter and can spread your wings. Forgiving doesn't mean restoring all rights, privileges, and responsibilities. This pardon is waving the white flag, but it isn't the right hand of fellowship. Some people don't deserve your presence, and it's your responsibility to guard your heart.

That's the work and the discipline of the higher life.

A scenario wherein you've done the work to forgive, but the person isn't of the mindset to receive may require some intercessory prayer and spiritual clearing of strongholds. One word of caution is that once you hold the space for forgiveness for someone, you don't earn the right to make them receive it nor expect them to show up differently. Regarding someone as blameless and being amicable toward them is a two-way street, and you may need to leave some time for the other person to catch up with that level of divinity. Again, that's the work and the discipline of the higher life.

Lastly, if you're having trouble dispensing mercy and forgiveness, dive more deeply into your psyche. Be more eager to explore what's real for you, and as your level of understanding of yourself expands, it will impact how you perceive others and the world around you.

The Early Days: Cussing Him Out as Therapy

Now there's the high road, the low road, and the 'bout-all-I-can-stand' road! Sometimes, I would fast, pray, and meditate, and my ex-husband still found a way to push that button way in the back of my mind. Today I understand how everything is always about me. There is usually a direct or indirect lesson, and yes, I understood that a few years into my divorce. However, early on, I found great pleasure in the occasional admonishment, also known as telling him off. At the time, it was healthier and more cathartic than other options. I don't recommend popping off at your ex because the rage that ensues could have terrible consequences, and remember, your energy matters!

This approach may be unexpected as many gurus insist that the goal is always to do the highest, most spiritual, and classy thing. But from time to time, after an onslaught of being ignored, disappointed, mistreated, and taken for granted, my ego would win. I would seize the opportunity to chasten and protest. Yes, there were times I decided to spew every foul, filthy, dirty word in my vocabulary.

I couldn't hold it in. I didn't have the tools to take the high road. My ex pissed me off and awakened the girl from Charlevoix and Van Dyke (the east side of Detroit).

If my frustration was bubbling over and I could not hang up the phone and go somewhere to pray and cry; if I couldn't be nice and say it wasn't a good time and that I'd call him back – when he dropped the ball yet again leaving me to clean up the mess, I cussed, fussed and vividly expressed my disdain of the offense. Then almost immediately, I felt better and moved on with my day - demure and gentle, I would be back to my graceful self.

Later, if I felt that the verbal lashing exceeded the offense, I would repent. But if I thought my sentiment warranted, I did not apologize, feel bad or ask for forgiveness.

While I realized the Bible did not condone the coarse language, I knew it taught that God chastised those he loved. I felt that when my ex-husband wasn't inclined to manage his performance, I had to call him out on some of his mess for my sanity and self-care.

It's like a player agreeing with a coach to perform a crucial play on the field but instead stands there, literally dropping the ball. The coach would admonish the player; explaining had the player followed through with the plan, the team could have won the game. Our family is the team, and it has structure.

If everyone does their part, we'll win. But if a player ruthlessly and carelessly sabotages the game, they deserve a challenge to their behavior.

Anger is not the sin, but how you express the anger may get you into rough waters. So, I felt that if I wasn't slashing tires, hitting or physically assaulting anyone, and the reprimand was warranted, I didn't transgress.

Even Jesus is known to turn over a few tables in the Temple!

I allowed my anger to help realign my ex-husband's priorities. I used my anger as a positive force to get us back on track. It's like there's a ship in a storm and the captain's guiding the crew. Sometimes the captain doesn't have time for gentle requests. It's a time to bark orders with no apology, or the ship is going to capsize. Unfortunately, some folks take religion and the superficial societal expectation of gender to deny reasonable, human emotions. I suspect this may be a lot more counter-productive than ever realized.

Again, I felt rather good after I got things out in the open and off my chest.

It may be time for us to rethink the imagery that we've been fed regarding how righteous people look and behave.

The woman in the Bible with the issue of blood had to be aware that she was working against severe restrictions for females, according to the religious order of the time.

But she was 'about that life!' She decided to forgo the niceties of polite society to effect change in her life.

The men and women of that time may not have been nearly as docile as we've been led to believe. As time went on, I began to see the excessive anger and arguing as a low energy approach to me. Yes, I would still voice my concerns but not as vehemently and from a place of self-love, not judgment. I'm not as ego-driven as I use to be and more focused on what's right instead of who's right. I realize I am a powerhouse, and my tongue doesn't need the energetic exchange as it did formerly, and I'm also aware of my Divine power to create the outcomes I desire by doing the inner work. I didn't know anything about this inner work and Divine power until a few years after the divorce, but as I learned better, I did better (that one is from our beloved Maya Angelou). Yes, we'd still argue, but the intensity of the blows dished out by both of us waned. We saw ourselves differently, and we saw each other differently as well. I'll go into more detail on showing up differently in Chapter 3.

The Curse of the Fairytale

• •

It's okay; you had a vision of what you wanted life to be and how your family would look. You honored most or all of your vows, but it didn't work out. Your vision didn't hold together, and I know it's heartbreaking, but can you deny that you willingly picked a man & walked the aisle to marry him despite red-flag behavior?

If you're born before the 2000s, you're amongst a population of women who were indoctrinated into the damsel archetype; she's in the pretty dress and gets rescued by the handsome Prince. So, when the opportunity presented itself, you saw what you needed to see and ignored what you didn't want to know so that you could have your fairytale.

If so, confess and own it. You picked the man and inadvertently picked the events that came along with him. Did you marry him because you felt you had limited choices? Ask yourself, did you ignore signs? Unanswered calls, pages with no callbacks (I'm from the beeper decade)? Were there questions of integrity that were presented early on but discounted?

I want to call that out because there's healing in recognizing how determined you may have been to have this fantasy. I needed to realize my ignorance and desperation due to daddy issues and unhealthy programming. I was looking for my daddy in these relationships with men because my dad wasn't there when I needed him to be—believing lies from split tongued men because I didn't have a standard to reference. My father didn't teach me how I should be treated. He taught me it was okay to be abandoned and that it's okay not to be taken care of, respected, treated lovingly, and adored. He taught me men don't honor and respect women, and women should not have any standards. It was through coaching, therapy, books, and courses that I learned about self-love and forgiveness. Books like Code of the Extraordinary Mind by Vishen Lakhiani empowered me to create beliefs out of nothing more than pure desire. In his book, Vishen says, create a rule that supports the person you want to be and the life you want to live. It doesn't matter if you have any basis for this rule, simply make it up and believe it. That's when I created fairy tales that served my highest and greatest good. More on that later, Now, it's also an excellent time to check your standards today. To do the inner work to shed limiting beliefs and truly take inventory of what you feel you're worthy of as a woman.

It's okay to make mistakes, but it's pretending you didn't make them that restrict you from being in flow. When we attract a man and pull him into our lives, wanting him to be something he's not, one way or another, we've got to face what we've done. We must become more fanatical with improving our own behavior than we are correcting anyone else's. On an episode of OWN TV's Iyanla Vanzant, Evelyn Lozada explained that she walked "…down that aisle…hopeful that [the relationship] would get better but deep down inside I knew it wasn't, but I did it anyway."

She went on to share that she "always knew that I wanted to have a family, but I was trying to have a family with the wrong person… [and] forcing it and accepting things that I can't even believe I accepted."

This dynamic of knowing something's off in a relationship but playing along is prevalent. Ladies, we deceive ourselves well before any man lies to us. We are far too eager to be double-crossed by a man, which is evident by our willingness to ignore red flags. We behave as if getting a ring is the price and proof of value, but it's just another hustle and scheme in far too many instances. Many women are competent at getting someone to propose but awful at qualifying a husband to marry.

With my marriage, I had limited guidance regarding men. I had no frame of reference to know what the standards and rules of engagement should be between a man and a woman. I had some guidance from men in my family – my Stepdad and male cousins managed to teach me a few things. But overall, I was over my head in marriage. Many women grow up hearing 'why buy the cow when you can get the milk for free' and hit their boyfriend with an ultimatum concluding that marriage will be him buying the cow. Rarely did I hear of a woman opting to regard the milk as a prized possession that only goes to the man who deserves it. She wasn't going to withhold the milk because another woman would do whatever she was unwilling to do, so her best bet was to get that ring.

Society does a great job of screwing up our heads as women but today is a new day. Information is available at the click of a button, so we're no longer limited to the teachings of momma, daddy, grandma, auntie, and the church. As an African American woman, I was curious about the spiritual practices of my ancestors. I often wonder what we lost as a culture when we were stripped of everything and brought to America. Thanks to the world wide web, I'm uncovering answers to questions regularly, and with every new insight, I experience a new level of ease, release, and power. A big part of the problem is we (women) are not reared to know our value, so we do not realize what we bring to the table and what we deserve in a partner. We are often too eager to make concessions that should never be made. Men are naturally willing and anxious to exchange the proper value for the time they get to share with us, but we put such a low value on it that we give our value away for free. Did you know that a man's testosterone level increases when he works for you? And that if you're easy, his levels drop? Men value the things they work for and getting to know you is worth working for in his eyes. I've met several men who were eager to rise to the occasion.

Whatever I required of them, they provided with a smile and seemed to appreciate me calling out the king in them. I could visibly see a shift in their posture as they took pride in winning me over. But wait, let me be clear, there were a few men who had no intentions of exerting any effort on my behalf, and one went so far as to say, "I can get the same thing from a woman and do nothing for her." This guy told me this early on, and yep, I dated him off and on for several years. Full transparency, I just had to forgive myself again for that decision as I'm writing this chapter, and it's been years since we dated. Forgiveness, surrender, and release is an ongoing thing. I'd go so far as to say it's a lifestyle.

Women are holy ground, and we deserve to be treasured rather than trampled over.

The privilege of calling and speaking with a woman on the phone has immense value. Yet many women don't believe that at all. As daughters, we aren't commonly taught the impact of our essence. Rarely are we let in on the secret that we change and transform the energy by merely walking into a room. We don't realize we are creators, healers, and even alchemists. Yes, with our breath, we're able to transmute and transcend situations and experiences. We don't realize women are igniters and carry a fire that can detonate as well as destroy.

One day I was in a crowded elevator, and when the doors opened, I walked out and towards the parking garage. A man who looked to be in his late 60's said, "Excuse me, you look very important; where do you work, or do you own this building?" I responded with a smile and a brief statement, and we went our separate ways. But I chuckled inside because I knew what he was experiencing in my presence. Although I didn't say a word, the energy exuding from me was intense, and that's precisely what the man witnessed. A few weeks before that encounter, I went through a two-week intensive confidence boot camp with my life coach Shanel Cooper-Sykes and

100 other women, and I learned the keys to accessing my Divine Goddess energy. Well, wait, let me be more accurate, I was made aware that I possessed a Divine Goddess energy, AND THEN I learned how to access it. My essence impacted him, and more importantly, it affected my ex. I was a new woman with him, and he didn't know what hit him. An evolved me awakened an evolved him.

I called up something great in him, and even when he didn't respond favorably, it no longer had a significant impact on me. He was also convicted by Spirit when he was out of alignment with our family's highest and greatest good and would often come back and apologize to me. The funny thing is I would've loved those apologies years ago, but at the time he started giving them, I didn't need them. His offenses no longer stuck to me. Yes, they'd sting, and we'd have some heated arguments here and there, but nothing like we did in the past before I tapped into my Divine Goddess energy. When we'd argue, I would be pissed and disappointed for a short period of time, but I had tools to process those feelings, and accordingly, I'd quickly snap out of it and ask myself, "What am I to become as a result of this? What is this presenting for me to learn? How is this helping me grow? What am I supposed to take away from this?" You see, I knew the Universe was set up to support me and would reflect whatever was stirring inside of me.

So, if I were out of alignment (#messy), I would attract a mess, and if I were whole, perfect, and complete, I'd be presented with situations that reflected that back to me as well. I also learned that I would be met with many lower energies because I was now aware of my power to heal and transform. People with grievances on the surface would appear to be directed towards me, but it was merely a call to love from me. Many childhood fairytales and fables fail to teach true feminine divinity and, instead, promote the helpless and the hero.

Women have been subliminally trained to hone their seduction skills more than to understand their value and what their presence means on a most basic level.

Today, if we could write new fairytales to depict life accurately, they would show the woman as powerful and full of magic. The magic wouldn't be exclusive to the fairy godmother or the evil witch. The woman would be her hero, and she'd be surrounded by people who reflect that love to her. The climax or scary part of the movie would be a villain coming in and trying to erase her memory, so she'd be unaware of how powerful she truly is. The handsome Prince would want to join kingdoms and build together. That's our truth; that's what our daughters need to see. Do I have any movie writers reading this? If so, call me, and let's flow this concept out and get it on the big screen for our children.

Okay, pulse check - Are you feeling anything stirring inside of you yet? This book is intended to awaken something that may have been dormant in you and now that you're aware of this information, you'll begin to be called to access it and operate from it. As you learn more about your energies, you'll be called to use them in various settings. It's a never-ending journey of evolving, but it's worth it. You're about to move into a deeper level of self-actualization where you'll begin to think everything critically, and nothing will be happenstance or meaningless. The seed will be planted in you, and there's no turning back. You'll be on a perpetual journey of self-mastery.

That fairytale program operates in even the most liberated amongst us. Stay ready to prune it whenever it pops up in your psyche. Life and love aren't fairytales; they're energy, a mindset, and a faith walk. Let go of the notion that you have to be Snow White to be loved and stop ignoring a lover's truth to embrace fantasy. The more whole you are as a woman, the healthier your engagement will be with your child's father. Remember, the goal is to provide a loving and healthy atmosphere for the children, which happens fluidly as your self-love level increases.

Taking Ownership

Take ownership and agency over your territory - your life. That begins with a simple, merciful act of self-forgiveness. We have to learn to love ourselves enough to forgive our sins. If we can't forgive ourselves, then we'll avoid admitting guilt to get around the pain and condemnation that brings.

> Lack of self-forgiveness only makes us
> master of the blame game.

I've witnessed the veracious path to freedom for myself as understanding why I made the choices I made. Once I unpacked that, I could shift to a new belief and behavior that supported me as I lived my life without repeating the same mistakes.

Here's the thing, as much as you may dislike your ex-husband now, he's your type.

> I believe a woman isn't attracted to a guy
> because she likes him; she's attracted
> because she thinks he's what she deserves.

I have a friend who told me the man who did the most damage in her life was someone she didn't even like when she first met him. She didn't find him attractive or very interesting. Soon enough, she convinced herself to date him and quickly excused his major red flags and poor treatment. Don't be surprised when your inner self-esteem issues come to the surface through choices that do not make logical sense.

Before my divorce, I persistently thought other men would be so much like my ex that there was no need for me to leave him since I'd only experience the same insanity with the next guy. That line of thinking was partially correct. Of course, there were other men out there just like my ex-husband, but the only trouble was that my mindset was more likely to attract *them* than the group of loving, loyal and monogamous men who were also available.

Consider there are lots of guys just like your ex out there, and if you don't do the work to correct your psyche and walk in your worth, you're likely to accept those guys when you meet them. You'll ignore their mess like you overlooked your ex's, and you'll fool yourself by falling asleep to fall in love.

I did what I did in love because I was unconscious, for the most part. I had to fast, pray and commit to a mindset regimen to get "woke" enough to dislodge the low standards set up in my mind throughout my life. The mindset work I've done, and continue to do, guards me against making poor choices in love in the future. As I meet men now, I intuitively know if they are for me or not. The powerful men profess their love for me almost immediately, and I love it! They are the ones I hold space for in my heart, and together we create something powerful. In the summer of 2019, I met two dynamic men and knew immediately we'd create magic together. Today Nate and Arias are my dear friends; we have a business together, work for each other, and have become family. I did the hard work to increase my magnetism and to become attractive on a cellular level. I attribute my healing and growth to my self-care rituals. The meditating, writing exercises, reading, therapy, all in tandem with me admitting my error, forgiving myself, and owning all my choices. This work is ongoing because healing never ends.

What Are Your Standards?

· ·

I heard Tony Robbins say, if you want more, raise your standard because, as a human, you'll never go lower than your standard. I don't know about you, but I didn't grow up listing out what my standards would be for love. I remember the men in The Plant (Chrysler Mound Road Engine Plant in Detroit) saying, "All these bitches better get along" and "I have window money, so if she gets mad at me and won't let me in, I'll break the front window and call Henderson Glass to come to fix it." We, everyone within earshot, laughed because we thought that was both funny and something to admire. Looking back, that was some of the most dysfunctional rhetoric I've ever heard. But that was the standard. The men with the money could have multiple women in different sections of the plant. I remember I saw a man spitting some A-One game to a new employee, and as I got closer to him, he told me, "I know you want to tell your girl on me, here, use my phone." Yes, he really said that to me and handed me his phone. I grew up in some extreme dysfunction - No wonder it took me until I hit my 40's to heal and create a new standard.

I believe there's a delicate balance between taking responsibility for your decisions versus unfairly blaming yourself for a divorce. Owning your part in things is crucial to your personal growth and maturity but owning your ex's piece is ridiculous. For instance, it's not your fault your ex repeatedly cheats, but it may be your fault if you continue to stay. If a man is an alcoholic and makes no attempt to get help to overcome his addiction for himself and his family, a woman's work is to safely make the hard choices for the family's sanity and safety.

Playing dumb is not only foolish, but it requires you to dumb down a bit. It requires you to pretend you didn't notice the red lipstick on the collar when everyone knows you did, and every concession is a loss of dignity and confidence.

> Men show who they are by what they do
> more than what they say. As a woman, your job is
> to listen to what they say and observe what they do.

It's a matter of personal agency. Another benefit of refusing to be a victim is that you develop decision-making muscles.

> When we remove the option of blaming others for failure, it empowers us to make a move, even make a mistake – but most importantly, to make a choice.

Sound decision-making is critical and operating in wisdom means refraining from being haphazard or hasty. Meditate, seek qualified counsel and mentors, pray, study books on the matter, then strategize your response and follow through. But please don't think you can solve a problem with the same mindset that created it.

Get some new information for a new perspective on maneuvering through the mud of facing your truths and making healthy decisions.

What are your standards?

What do you deserve?

What do you desire to experience in a love relationship?

These are questions that, if answered, serve as your north star. Follow them without compromise and watch how your relationships transform.

In coaching different women and exchanging notes with sisters for years, life is about intellect, intuition, and the confidence to make reliable decisions. You will eventually look for internal confirmation more than external, knowing that you have the confidence to grapple with options and make the smart choice. You may hire experts and counselors, but you will also need the wisdom to know how to use the information given to build and grow your territory.

An empowered woman is also impervious to the familiar baby-baby-please cycle that keeps couples on an endless treadmill of breaking up only to make up. When a man is begging to reconcile, a wounded woman will want to take that as an indication that reconciliation is in order. I understand how good it feels to see the man grovel and beg for a second, third, or fourth chance. I also know how good we women are at *pretending* to be fed up. We often play as if we are seriously leaving this time as we go through all the motions.

I heard a story wherein a woman even leased a new apartment and moved out only to gloat a little and get his attention. But she was back for more with her husband a few short months later, having wasted a security deposit and moving costs. Some of us may be addicted to the drama, the break-up, and the begging phase when he's so attentive and groveling.

That's low vibrational, and we're operating higher than that at this phase of our journey. So, that being said, we are now addicted to dignity, confidence, and being treated with honor. That's the standard.

That's a woman's work – to build self-esteem and do the mindset work that supports productive choices rather than desperate concessions.

When someone we love makes a mistake, repentance is evident by submitting to higher checks and new standards. Suppose things go from begging and pleading to a show of frustration without any demonstration of tangible change. In that case, things quickly go back to business as usual, it's a game, and the woman is playing right along, being equally accountable in the farce.

His begging doesn't mean he's improving his efforts. I admit the groveling can be entertaining as an interesting ploy, but there must be more to justify reconciliation. Women pretend that pleading is something significant, but many women know, in their hearts, that the man isn't different.

Childhood Trauma

Do you have childhood trauma or distress? Were you somehow able to survive the ordeal and go on to leave the environment and situation? Many women go through their lives doing their best to forget that childhood trauma ever occurred. However, their poor life choices prove that the trauma has left its mark and become a driving force and barrier to their progress and purpose.

Consider whether you're harboring major trauma in your body and psyche.

A tendency to make poor and harmful choices is a red flag that you may be making decisions out of desperate beliefs developed years ago. Ask yourself why you have specific belief systems in place, especially as it pertains to love, romance, and marriage? Question everything! Did someone leave you, say something to you or touch you inappropriately? Is there something that happened in your life that caused you to make certain assessments? If so, it's an opportunity to seek help, whether it's an energy healer, a therapist, or someone trained in understanding how to move that energy to help you process and clear it. If there are thoughts of suicide or chronic fatigue, see a licensed therapist to help you get yourself to a better place. Our bodies hold all trauma, and it doesn't go anywhere on its own.

Time may heal all wounds, but it doesn't heal trauma.

Arguably, time weaponizes trauma like a stealth missile, making it barely noticeable until it explodes. When we hold distress instead of processing it, the trauma becomes a personality and another voice - an ego in your psyche. It's wise to get help when facing a divorce in general but consider the value in getting help with matters beyond the matter of divorce.

Trauma gets entrenched. It becomes so deep-seated that some women fail to realize how much we protect it. We refuse to approach certain topics, won't deal with them effectively, and criticize anyone who tries to dig up the trauma's roots. Trauma needs you to focus on other people's mess and leave yours alone to fester, which is why we compulsively criticize, gossip, and blame others. Trauma needs to be held sacred and unchallenged. So much so that picking up this book about amicable divorce quickly gets misconstrued as a book about getting your ex-husband to be nice.

But if you believe that having an amicable, co-parenting, post-divorce relationship can only occur if your ex-husband gets in line and does *his* work, you might be delusional. It takes two.

This book's concepts become far-fetched when you fail to face your ghosts and demons – refusing to do *your* work. This book is about doing the self-work and clearing the trauma that fueled the choices that got you here. Take a deep breath and receive the task of refusing to let old beliefs and distress impair your current perspective and flexibility. Use the tools in this book to challenge the sensitive topics, seek counsel, and safely clear emotional damage. That is the way to heal yourself and be a vessel of healing for your family.

The films *Emotions* by Frazer Bailey and the documentary entitled *Heal* by Kelly Noonan offer great insights regarding the harnessing of emotions. There are many exceptional resources on the internet, do your research, and invest in what resonates with you. For women who are not averse to Eastern modalities, acupuncture and Reiki may prove helpful, as well. In my experience, practitioners who specialize in a mind, body, and spirit approach have proven to be the most beneficial. I enlist the help of Eastern therapies. I find that those modalities work well for me. I encourage you to find what works for you and never stop exploring and researching.

My daughter communicated great satisfaction with having someone listen to her during grief counseling sessions with a licensed therapist after her dad (my ex) transitioned from this life. My oldest son gravitated towards Reiki and calisthenics. And my youngest son practiced fasting. Ultimately, it's all about realizing we hold trauma in our bodies and taking action to clear it. Therapies help us get the owner's manual to our bodies and identify the root of our lives' problems.

Get woke and plugged in but be sure to steer clear of mindless religion and the traditions of men.

Consider helpful references that include the Bible. Authors like Wayne Dyer, Joe Dispenza, Eckhart Tolle, Marianne Williamson, and Bruce Lipton, minsters like T.D. Jakes and Michael Bernard Beckwith and thought leaders like Oprah Winfrey with her *Super Soul Sunday* broadcasts. Setting a regimen of study, personal analysis, and treatments with professionals will help take you out of your traumatized paradigm and offer a more profitable perspective.

EXERCISE 2.1

Mental Renewal
List Your Standards

Action: Think about yourself and what you truly desire.

List 25 desires. There are no rules, restrictions, or requirements. The only caveat is this list must be your true desires. Not what someone else thinks you should have, or what you feel you're limited by.

- Turn on instrumental music – Jazz, Meditation Tones, Chakra Healing Tones – You'll find several to choose from on YouTube, Spotify or Pandora

- Smile while writing (even if you feel ridiculous).

List 25 or more of your desires. Use extra paper if you need to.

_____

_____

_____

_____

_____

_____

_____

_____

_____

_____

_____

_____

_____

_____

_____

_____

_____

_____

_____

_____

_____

_____

Mindset Mastery Exercise

Are All Men Dogs?

A man can be a dog or a god. A woman can be a dog or goddess. It is a matter of consciousness. Culture, childhood trauma, and life experiences also help determine how a man or woman presents themselves to the world.

If it's true that we attract what we believe, it serves us well to transmute any condemnation of men as a group.

There may be several wonderful men who would love you properly, but you will repel them with any persistent bitterness and low expectation.

It may be challenging, in the beginning, to learn and master the exercises in this book. Nonetheless, as you persevere with the training, you will transcend the belief that men are not trustworthy. You will be able to change your point of attraction to draw into your existence more eligible, viable candidates. Even if it's not your intention to jump into a relationship at this time, by clearing your thoughts regarding men, you'll have healthier interactions with them personally and professionally.

As for the thoughts of regret and assertions that you picked the wrong guy, know that you made your decisions based on the information and perspective you had at the time. Let go of the anxiety and regret about things. Begin to believe in love again by loving yourself by being sweet, kind, and gentle with you. Perfection is not the goal of life. Ever evolving, always learning, and progressing is the goal. Self-mastery, releasing negative energy, forgiving, teaching others, and finding joy in life is the goal.

Despite all you've endured, you are highly favored and immeasurably blessed because everything brought you to this moment when you hold this book. Now, regardless of what got you here, you are the one changing things for the better for you and your family.

Are we attracted to the bad boy or broken man because we don't have an accurate view of ourselves?

I am the first to raise my hand, I use to be intrigued by the bad boy, but today, that type repulses me. I am not fond of anyone who resembles mystery or unattainable. I believe it's because of the understanding that I have about who I am, and I'm aware of my purpose for being in this incarnation. I don't have time, energy, or interest in focusing my attention on figuring out a man. Today, it's the dynamic men who are an open book that I find attractive, the ones who want to include me, who want to be where I am and who dive into my business's operations and me into his. I realize it's vital for my partner to have a similar or complementary life calling. We don't have to do everything together, but it means there is no wall up with a sign on it that says don't enter. I'm not concerned about loyalty because we're in this for higher reasons, and our connection is spiritual.

Author and thought leader, Eckhart Tolle, mentions some couples are drawn to each other only because their respective pain-bodies complement each other in a conversation with Oprah.

There's more in play than we may realize – from childhood upbringing, trauma, and self-esteem, we find the men who confirm our expectations.

Consider that obsessing over the mentally unhealthy population of men may only serve to distract us from connecting with the healthy population of men. So, the viable question is, how can you attract healthy men who have mastered the practice of transparency and vulnerability in an intimate relationship? The answer is mental renewal. We don't attract what we want; we attract who we are. That being said, it is wise to embody your true essence before getting back into the dating world. But if you do happen to jump out there before zeroing in on your true self, you'll know by what you attract. Try to shake your head, laugh it off, get back in your sacred space, and continue doing your work.

(See the Environment section for a description of a sacred space)

EXERCISE 2.2

Mental Renewal
What we focus on, we attract. Release thoughts about men that no longer serve you and rewrite your new beliefs.

Action:

• In Column A, write the negative traits you were taught to believe about men by your elders, society, etc.

• In Column B, write the traits you desire to experience in a man

  o Example:

Negative Teachings: (Column A)	I desire to experience a man who is: (Column B)
Unfaithful	Faithful
Lazy	Driven
Slow	Brilliant
Negative Teachings: (Column A)	I desire to experience a man who is: (Column B)

Tip: DO NOT SKIP THIS EXERCISE. There's power in writing. Write what you desire – this is a step in manifesting. Even if you don't feel worthy, write it. Even if you don't believe a caring, honest, faithful, loving, compassionate, protective, brilliant, and supportive man exists today, just write it.

You may experience a feeling or a shift in your energy as you complete this exercise. Write some notes here to describe what came up for you or what you experienced.

Notes/Questions/Revelations:

_____

_____

_____

_____

_____

_____

_____

_____

_____

_____

_____

_____

_____

Mindset Mastery Exercise

Three

Protecting Our Legacy

"My cup runneth over...
What comes out of the cup is for y'all...
What's in the cup is mine."
—Iyanla Vanzant

When flying on an airplane, flight attendants give a safety speech to the passengers. In the event of an emergency, oxygen masks will drop from overhead. The attendant advises the passengers to secure their mask over their face first, then assist children. As mothers, it's instinctive for us to put our children's needs ahead of our own. I believe nature intended for it to be that way to some degree. I do feel, however, as with everything, finding balance is paramount. As mothers, we regularly sacrifice for our children. Many of us began at the point of conception by offering our body, sleep, and energy to make room for this new life. Being a mother can be summed up as the ultimate sacrifice in my book. That being said, I do believe many women could benefit from a refueling of sorts – a commitment to sacred self-care (see the Lifestyle section for details). We don't run out of the house with a cell phone that has a 20% battery life. However, day after day, mothers worldwide jump out of the bed and manage their lives with a body and mind flashing low battery. With maybe 20% battery life, we get the kids off to school, go to work, serve as our family's personal Uber/Lyft service, grocery shop, cook meals, check homework, encourage the kids to share parts of their day so we can make sure everything is good with them, wash a load of laundry, squeeze in a girlfriend chat, scroll through Facebook and Instagram, look for sleep with every fiber of our being only to finally find it at 1:30 am. It starts all over again at 5:30 am the next day. The to-do list isn't going away; it's a lifestyle. But there is a way to refuel our energetic battery, so we operate closer to 100%. When is the last time you've felt fully charged? How would you show up in the critical areas of your life energized spiritually, emotionally, and physically? You would be on fire!

Giving from a place of abundance and not out of lack or obligation. The entire world benefits from a woman who operates from the fullness of her true self, including HER! I believe each woman is a whole universe. Yes, an individual woman is an entire universe. With that, each woman has access to everything she needs in the present moment – another way of saying this is: there is nothing a woman needs that she doesn't have access to. #period. Nonetheless, when we operate out of a deficient space, our egos run the show. Instead of flowing through life poised and graceful, we clunk around, with a scowl as our RBF (resting bitch face) as we check all of the boxes on our to-do list.

Your legacy deserves what you will emit and create as you operate in your fullness. Your children deserve a mother who is whole and in touch with what fulfillment looks like for herself. Tap into the fullness of who you are as you consciously choose to operate with a divine knowing of your power.

Seeing the Big Picture

Child-rearing requires us to remain authentically true to the big picture. We gain when we're teachable rather than adversarial.

Everyone wins when the goal isn't to find the easiest or quickest way to do things but rather find the best way for the group. It is not for us to pursue our way, our Ex's way, or even to appease the kids. It's for us to keep our focus on the big picture, the desired outcome, and make decisions that get everyone as close to that destination as possible. Now sometimes that means you have the best idea, but it also means sometimes you don't. Considering the perspectives of your ex and your children could help you strengthen your bond with them. Everyone wants to know they matter, and they're heard. I'm not suggesting you have to concede to their approach to solving a problem, but when you give them a platform to be heard and seen, it conveys to them you value them individually as a person and as a member of your family. Remember, a family isn't a dictatorship. Each person has a unique perspective and may offer a different approach to solving a problem. I found it very beneficial to take a step back and ask myself, "20 years from now, what will be the most important takeaway from this present moment, and what decision can I make right now that is in the interest of the big picture?" #legacy. This exercise helped me evolve from being a control freak ex-wife and mother who is always right into a fair and easily approachable woman who appreciates her family's voice. As I shifted, I noticed my family shifting. When my ex-husband felt respected, heard, and valued, he showed up less aggressive and adversarial. In short, he put his dukes down because my energy was disarming. When the children saw us flowing in the dance of co-parenting, they relaxed and became lighter. As parents, we lifted the burden of our dysfunctional relationship from our children's shoulders, which allowed them to be at ease. To be joyful, relaxed, and whole. When I operated from a space of love and acceptance, my ex showed up differently in our relationship, and I became a magnet that attracted the best of him (most days, don't get me wrong, we still argued, just not as often or as brutal). The light that flowed through me infected my ex and then our children. Remember earlier; I mentioned a woman is an entire universe; this is an example of what I meant.

As Vivian changed, everyone around Vivian changed. Vivian couldn't show up as a whole light being and continue to be treated the same as when she was operating out of fear.

When I was judgmental, controlling, and a victim, I attracted events to support me in my continued effort to be judgmental, controlling, and a victim. This mindset was taxing on my energy, and it never felt good, but it was all I knew. So how did I learn a different approach? What sparked my curiosity to find a new way of living? During a session with my spiritual astrologer, Aluna Michaels, she recommended I buy Dr. Joe Dispenza's book, Breaking the Habit of Being Yourself. This book taught me that neurons that fire together wire together, so to have a different set of outcomes, I had to have different thoughts. Dr. Joe D. teaches beliefs are thoughts you keep thinking, and those beliefs dictate choices, choices dictate behaviors, and the result of a set of behaviors translates to your life. I love Dr. Joe Dispenza; check him out on YouTube and get his books. You'll create a new you.

I began to listen and hear our children from a place of self-love, and they could sense they were valued and heard. Hearing them became easier for me as I healed. As I released the story of the victim, I released hopelessness. I became whole and full, meaning I had something substantial to give and a harmonious place from which to share. Another quick tip is to recognize our children's humanity. The human condition is flawed on a good day and corrupt on its worse. The idea that our kids are little angels serves no one, and divorce sometimes serves as the perfect opportunity for children to learn resilience #shithappens.

For the first five years of my divorce, my children played both their dad and me like a fiddle. Yes, they were suffering, but they quickly discovered a way to position themselves for success. My three children formed their first mastermind group with a single interest in forwarding their agenda. Collectively, they mastered the art of manipulation and leveraged it regularly. One day a good friend of mine came over to visit, and as we chatted, she watched the kids in action. After a few minutes, she said, "Do you realize your kids are master manipulators?" I looked puzzled. She went on to say, "The good thing is they are strategic, and they've tapped into flipping the worse situation into one that benefits them. The bad thing is they keep putting you and your ex at odds, which keeps you both defending and competing." #lightbulbmoment

Just Because You Took an "L"

During the divorce, I use to think to suffer a loss by my ex-husband's hand meant I had to retaliate against him every chance I got. That quickly became exhausting and as I began to appreciate healthy versus unhealthy energy and karma, I began to refrain from obsessing over every win and battle. At first, it took disciplining the flesh and ego to give up the vendetta.

I felt I had been wronged and was entitled to retribution.

But eventually, I gave up the feeling that I was entitled to the *Big Payback* so James Brown would have to find someone else to strut to that soundtrack. I know it's tempting but adopting a vengeful spirit after being cheated-on, duped or abandoned is a sure way to sabotage your present moment fulfillment, future happiness and possibly your kid's childhood. #aintnobodygottimeforthat

Children are not responsible for helping you win or have the last word on things. Trust me, being petty doesn't improve your position in life so resist ego led moments that tempt you to put your kids in the middle of your battle with your ex. You may be thinking, "He uses the kids to spite me all the time!" Whelp, you're reading this book now and that means you're ready to try something different to get different results. Effective immediately, you no longer operate in a tit for tat model. It is of great benefit to be mindful of how you frame the things you say and do. Ask yourself often, "What is my intention?" The answer to this question will help steer you towards your desired outcome. Remember, everything you say or do is a seed. A seed that you're planting in your very own garden of life.

It took me several years and countless tears to understand that getting your child to empathize and rally like a cheerleader on your behalf is unfair to your child. Your children have two parents and it's unfair to make one the hero and one the villain. They love you both regardless of who does more for them physically, mentally or financially. "Your daddy ain't shit" is not a comment your children need or want to hear come from you. Don't require their loyalty or encourage them to conspire with you to help you win wars. They are children who just want both parents to love them and to be happy. Have you ever wondered why some folks profess to love someone and then proceed to hurt and manipulate that person? Makes you wonder what their exposure was to love growing up.

Divorce can inadvertently become a training ground for children to learn deception and conspiracy.

Kids are always observing and learning. We teach them how to process events and manage emotions through our words and actions. I have an exercise that I do with my kids maybe once or twice a year. I take one kid out for a ride, maybe to go grab a bite, and while we're en route, I ask them what would their response be if a counselor, reporter or someone they viewed as an authority, asked them, "What words do you use to describe your Mother? Is your mother a happy woman or sad? Does your mother love her life or does she seem to hate it?" Warning, these questions prompt children to be transparent and share what they see from their perspective. When my middle child Robert was 12 or 13, I asked him these questions. He said I (his mother) was worried and frustrated, sometimes happy but mostly stressed out. This was an eye opener for me, and it was after that conversation I began to carefully observe how I showed up. It was excruciatingly difficult to be humane and forgiving early on. I know these pages are full of "take the high road" suggestions, but please be gentle with yourself if you're not there yet. This mindset shift is a process. It's an unlearning of everything we've been taught and on a biological level, it's shifting you out of fight or flight mode.

Children are always watching what we do. They are sensitive to energy and know when words don't match actions. Consider using your separation and divorce as a training ground for your kids to learn how to be humane, forgiving, self-affirming, and sovereign. Teaching children all humans are trying to figure this thing called life out and everyone is doing their best based on the information they have at the time. Try reassuring them they're covered by their human mom and human dad despite their flaws and more importantly by, and in the image of the Creator, Infinite Intelligence, God, therefore they lack no-thing.

Fear of Failing the Kids

From time to time, my son Robert (19) would describe one of his problems, and my ex-husband and I would tease him by mockingly rattling off descriptions of some "real problems." He and I were born and raised in Detroit, and we had real problems growing up, but our kids were suburban kids, so the struggle was not comparable in our eyes. Our kids were raised in Plano, Texas, and Robert would push back at our dismissive attitude, saying, "Well, no, I don't have Detroit problems, I have Plano problems and my problems are real." He went on to explain that his problems were still troubling regardless of the caliber or location. At the time, we failed to realize the lesson our son was trying to teach. We were minimizing what he went through based on *our* standard of struggle. In hindsight, we dropped the ball on providing space for him to witness us respect his issue. I'm shaking my head just writing this because now that he's older, he sees why we clown him, but at the time, it wasn't the healthiest way to parent. #whenyouknowbetteryoudobetter

Eventually, I learned to embrace that pain-was-relative and that everyone had the right to decide how they felt about an experience. In retrospect, I'm grateful my son managed to navigate specific problems despite the failure of the support he deserved. While I'm much more empathetic today, I have learned to pray that all my kids would have other positive influencers and mentors to support them, especially in the areas I neglect.

**I asked God to show up in the people
that my children encountered.**

I knew being a mother wasn't a magic trick. I didn't get superpowers and 24/7 ESP as a result of giving birth. At one point, when my kids were very young, we were in the kitchen, and they thought it was funny to call me by my first name. I played along for a little while, and it alleviated some of the overbearing dynamics between parent and child. While I know this line of thinking is not for everyone, I believe that there are instances where too much stock is put into people who had sex that resulted in birthing new human beings. Our children come to this planet with their guidance manual, called intuition, spiritual insight, emotions, and intellect. As adult parents, we are commissioned to keep them safe, help them hone those skills, and avoid unnecessary pitfalls. I don't pretend to know it all and instead actively create contingencies for the times that I may drop the ball as a parent. After they played around with calling me Vivian a few times, the humor noticeably waned, and I could feel them as they nestled back into the comfort of uttering the word "Mom".

Since I am not my kid's god, and I will get a lot of things wrong, I encourage my children to give feedback, especially when they suspect I'm doing something less than optimally. While I require respect in their method of communicating, I don't restrict their insight. I believe parents must be brave enough to respect their children's opinions. Often, exhausted and overwhelmed parents give themselves a passing grade in child-rearing when, in fact, they could use some coaching and support.

Be open to correction and build a village of qualified help to nurture your babies.

They Ain't Gon' Die

I have a hard time pushing my perspective on people, but everything I'm sharing is something that I've tried, and it worked for me. I want to remind you that I'm not a therapist, doctor, or counselor. What I am is a woman who thrived post-divorce despite the odds. What I am is a mother of three dynamic humans who I am humbly proud of. Their character, critical thinking, spiritual acumen, and overall flow delight my soul! That's why I share this and offer perspectives to consider. This stuff worked for me, so take what resonates with you, leave what doesn't. Nothing is one size fits all.

Resist the temptation to be God to your babies. It is not your role to be your kids' everything. The mother is a vessel and steward - God is the Source. Be authentically true to the big picture. So, what's the big picture? For me, it was to know how to work *with* God/Source/Creator to get my physical, spiritual, and emotional needs met, and then learn how to cultivate that skill in my children.

The big picture is legacy, leaving a tradition
and a family line that navigates this
world system – no matter what happens or
what's thrown in the mix.

There's a very complicated, pseudo-scientific phrase that I employ when I've done the best that I can do, but things don't quite come together concerning the kids. Now get ready because it's profound:

They Ain't Gon' Die!

I used this sentiment whenever I needed to release the impulse to fight an unnecessary battle. Whenever my ex-husband would do something that ran crossways of our agreement concerning the kids, I had to learn to pick battles wisely.

The thing that helped me do that was releasing
myself from the obsession of creating
perfect experiences for my kids according
to my definition of perfect.

Our children are relatively durable and will, in most cases, be just fine. Of course, the caveat is that some children are gravely sensitive to food, sleep schedules, medications, etc. Mapping out a daily plan for those children is crucial, and there is an obvious need to enforce stricter boundaries. However, a vast majority of us have reasons to be overflowing with gratitude because our children are resilient, healthy, and willing to go with the flow.

When tempted to correct someone's behavior or argue a case, breathe a long cleansing breath and consider whether a fight is really necessary.

For example, a model scenario:

Your ex-husband routinely returns the kids home to you very late even though you've asked him to return them at an earlier time so you can wind them down and get them to bed for school the next day. Time and time again, he drops them off as late as 10 or 11 PM, and sometimes they arrive starving.

You have the option to declare another war, or you may glean a few lessons and keep it moving.

Lesson 1: admit the children **are not** starving – just a little hungry, and a quick snack and glass of water could do the trick.

Self-mastery requires us to refrain from hyperbole when angry. Exaggeration encourages over-reaction, so calm down to see more of the truth.

Lesson 2:

The Ayurvedic health system, which includes intermittent fasting, is one of the oldest whole-body protocols – developed thousands of years ago in India. I'm not suggesting you try it, but I am bringing it up because it's a lifestyle choice that has proven beneficial by helping the digestive system, immune system, and more. Also, studies have shown that late night eating is an undetected and significant problem for many people.

So, this scenario whereby your ex returns the children without feeding them is a spontaneous opportunity to teach your children how to promote health in their bodies, even when it requires denying appetite and desire. Of course, this doesn't apply if your child has special dietary needs. Again, what I'm sharing isn't one size fits all. So, if your child will get sick if they don't eat according to a set routine, by all means, stand firm on that and don't waiver.

Welcome opportunities to teach our children
to manage their impulses & appetites! Amen?

Lastly, many families perform religious fasting rituals, requiring the children to participate on some level. And fasting to keep the peace and get along is a comparable sacrifice.

Lesson 3:

While proper sleep is vital, there are times when we are over-scheduled. Many children routinely stay up longer than is healthy or fidget in bed for hours before falling asleep.

It's an on-going challenge, and children could benefit from being taught how to manage on the days that they get less rest than usual.

Considering the above scenario, do you see how revising your internal perspective gives you more power over the situation than exerting force outwardly to control your ex-husband's power?

EXERCISE 3.1

Action: **Write the behavior you want to address in your ex.** *(for example: my ex drops the kids off late.)*

Behavior: ....

Action: Write the purpose and/or benefits for addressing your ex-husband's behavior. *(for example: my Ex will know how much the lateness bothers me.)*

1. ....

2. ....

3. ....

Tip: If the benefit of checking a behavior serves everyone in the group, perhaps there's a need for discussion. But if the benefit is for you and is likely to cause more contention in the group, consider letting go.

> *Perspective: Consider whether another argument about the matter will encourage your ex to respond with a more desirable behavior, for example, dropping off the kids on time?*

Tip: If you choose confrontation, consider leading the conversation with the context of how the children will benefit. Read Crucial Conversations by Al Switzler, Joseph Grenny, and Ron McMillan for help cultivating this skill.

Rock & Hard Places

In the case of gross neglect and behavior from other parties, you will need planning, strategy, contingencies, agencies, allies, and Divine intervention.

I am not in a position to advise regarding issues of child welfare and abuse. However, I do encourage you to search out and recruit every resource and support known to man to help you and your children overcome your challenges.

In many cases, there are professional workers and agencies specializing in what you are experiencing, and they can be a source of advice, planning, and necessary comfort. Don't give up; rally your team of legal, medical, psychological, and/or other professionals and also find a therapeutic source for your personal care, as well as your children. Don't minimize your healing process. Take the time and enlist the resources to help you heal, clear out the anxiety and transmute the energy of what you are regularly experiencing, or you'll be unable to be a source of strength for your family.

Remember that strength isn't standing
on your own; it's receiving the
flow & provision of help from God's vessels.

We all know there may be circumstances too sensitive or complicated to approach directly with your ex-husband, so you may need to place little angels and allies as a hedge of protection for the kids when you're not around. I realize that for some of our sisters in the global family worldwide, the choices are like selecting between a rock and a hard place. But women are master strategists; we can usually come up with ways to get around a rocky boulder or two.

Concerning Divine intervention, be sure to get in the creative mindset with the exercises at the end of this chapter. Complete the exercises with the understanding that you are calling on the Creator to provide a nurturing environment for your kids wherever they go, including in the care of your ex-husband. The nurturing environment may come by way of your ex-husband's family members, even a girlfriend, so acknowledge and give gratitude that your help comes from many sources.

> Find comfort in the thought that your
> kids are the Creator's kids too,
> and with a little coordination,
> they may be protected & inspired
> wherever they go
> in the world.

Using Your Tools

When a divorce occurs, children tend to have to grow up quickly as they are forced to deal with some situations that are not always wholesome. Our prayers are not cotton-candy fairytales but weaponry and tools to navigate pitfalls and weather the storms with the least amount of injury and bitterness. Positive thinking is about finding the light within the darkness, and the idea that life should always be rainbows and unicorns is just lazy.

We're on the planet to learn lessons,
and sometimes the heat and pressure of
life create a power in us that makes us
ready for the world.

As such, divorce is a great training ground for mastering how to strategize, doing what you can, and then releasing control. You are responsible for creating the life you desire but understand that you never walk alone on the journey.

Stepping into your creative power doesn't mean
becoming God, but it means becoming
co-creator with that Force.

This dynamic is in play concerning your children more than anything.

Since you are not around for everything your children experience, especially when they're with their dad, you may take solace in tapping into that supernatural and Divine Force. This tool will come in handy as they get older. Create a regular practice of prayer over them, asking that the voice of God is loud in their ear, especially when you're absent. While you'll teach them wisdom and how to follow their inner guidance, you'll also activate a covering over them and cause them to have seemingly supernatural favor too.

I encourage having regular conversations with your children. As a Mom, I prefer to leave things to strategy rather than chance. Keeping your head in the sand about something is not faith but denial, so deal with things as they come up. As shocking as they may be, face it head-on and remember, this too shall pass.

When a conversation with the children reveals something alarming, resist the feeling to be dramatic. If you fuss or fly off the handle, the kids may be triggered to fight, or flight and this could shut down the lines of communication. I learned I would rather hear from my kids than not and making them feel uncomfortable is a quick way to teach them to shut down and refrain from revealing things to you. Consider this, when you're livid, and out of control about something concerning them, the children can no longer hear your words. They are merely trying to survive the episode. They are no longer absorbing the lessons that you hope to impart to keep them safe. Again, practicing meditation helps master calm and train the monkey mind and body to settle down on command. Meditation was crucial to my success as a divorcee and single mom. See Chapter 7 for beginning steps to meditating.

Your meditation practice is a rehearsal for the mind and body, training them to snap into calm focus regardless of stimulus.

If the child is very young, there's less autonomy for the little guy, and you'll have to pray all the more. As they get older, you may equip them with some strategic preparation regarding visiting their dad.

When the child returns from a visit with their father, resist the desire to interrogate.

Try to have a conversation that's easy and organic, or you may inadvertently train the child to keep secrets or feel conflicted about what to share with you and their dad.

Remember, if they share some ugly truth with you and you become furious and call your ex, starting another war, they will begin to filter their conversations. Practice improving your strategy and disciplining your flesh enough to keep things light. Set your intention to master calmness and self-control. Tap into your meditation to strengthen that skill. Detach yourself enough to be strategic with your kids.

Don't be scared, and don't be a victim.
Be a co-creator with God.

The whole purpose is to give your child space to process, heal, and learn from whatever they experience.

Refrain from addressing things defensively but speak to it in context and on the level of that child's understanding. Be ready to give an account for accusations against you made by the other camp. There may be times when things get a little heated, and your ex-husband may inadvertently or purposely reveal things that disparage your character with the kids.

Since some of the claims may be true about your character, mistakes, etc., you'll need to already be at peace with it, having already forgiven yourself.

I've heard of instances wherein an ex-spouse reveals to the children that the other parent wanted to abort them or that the mother had an affair. If those sorts of disclosures are possible and especially if they are entirely accurate, do your emotional work and personal forgiveness exercises so you can resist being defensive. Resist the temptation to pull rank as a parent, claiming that you don't owe a child an explanation. That defensive yet cowardly response can sever trust and respect in ways that impact the child's perspective of you. This scenario demonstrates the importance of self-forgiveness and being perpetually at peace with your choices, especially your mistakes. Remember, the child is looking for safety and love. They possibly need to be reassured that you love them, and you're always there for them, and regardless of how things play out, you're their mom, and you love being their mom.

Be ready to address your issues in a way that doesn't make matters worse.

Use every opportunity to teach your children lessons in forgiveness for yourself and others. Use every opportunity to convey the valuable lesson of how to embrace your shortcomings and past behavior.

The strategy could prove to be a balance between strength, humility, and independence with an ability to co-create with God. Cover your children and aim to give them a foundation for the truth and life lessons they haven't yet mastered.

EXERCISE 3.2

Quick Prayer

Take a picture of this prayer or write your own and take a picture with your cell. Set reminders to look at this prayer **5** times throughout your day. Tape a copy to your mirror in the bathroom!

Speak the Prayer Several Times Daily

I appreciate that my children are surrounded by love and are in nurturing environments wherever they go. My children are spiritually aware of their energy and have common sense. They are protected, safe, supported, uplifted, and loved.

I appreciate our village of supporters and nurturers, for the people who eagerly give my children wise counsel and keep a watchful eye over them when they are in their presence.

I appreciate that my children know they are loved, and their hearts are filled and overflowing with fulfillment, faith, and excitement about life.

I appreciate being full of energy & vitality, and I naturally provide the fun-loving, nurturing, soft heart, a listening ear, and attentive spirit my children need from me.

(Add to This Prayer in the Space Below or Write Your Own)

_____

_____

_____

_____

_____

_____

_____

_____

_____

_____

_____

_____

_____

_____

_____

_____

_____

_____

_____

_____

_____

_____

_____

_____

_____

_____

_____

_____

_____

Mindset Mastery Exercise

Environment

• •

I have a sacred space in my home – a corner of the house intentionally designed to be tranquil with candles, pillows, essential oils, etc. When the children were due to return home from their Father, I would sit there having already prayed, meditated, and breathed into that space of calm. When the kids came in to kiss me hello, I was in the best position to manage what they had to tell me about their visit. The details on how to begin meditating are in Chapter 7.

I'd have soft, quiet music playing, and they often voluntarily sat on the floor with me to chat. The children may not have even realized how much the music and environment helped support serenity or how my posture and facial expression communicated safety and calm. I deliberately set the tone to receive them in peace.

> Consider that your ability to handle even the worse
> news hinges on how you set things up in your favor.

Create an environment that supports the best outcomes. If you want peace in the home, prepare a place for it. Refrain from treating peace like something you call on in the heat of the moment; instead, consider it a lifestyle.

Peace is a practice!

When you build your village of support for your children, lining-up the teachers, mentors, and professionals to help them live their best lives, your work is not done.

Developing the people and the places that support your child-rearing effort is necessary, but there's one more "P" in the plan. The word "practice" is equal in importance.

When you marvel at someone's ability to stay calm in a difficult moment, you are witnessing the fruits of their labor from their private spiritual practice. It may seem as though they simply chose to be at peace despite a moment of chaos, but it's more likely that they prepared for success many weeks prior. That moment of peace within the chaos is proof that they lower their high beta brain waves (meditated) weeks ago. When you see someone passing their life's trials with flying colors; they wrote in their journals for that, they read books and studied scriptures and sage wisdom for it, they did multiple writing meditations of forgiveness, and they ate more wholesome food for it; they did *their* spiritual, mindful, and physical work for it.

Do the work to train your mind and body to feel anger but refuse a sinful response. If you fail to practice peace before you need it, you'll get alarming news from the kids or about a situation, and it'll already be too late to get in front of it, emotionally. If you haven't done the spiritual work, exorcised your demons, and trained your flesh, your reaction could have a greater chance of making matters even worse. If you build an environment of peace in your physical space and create an internal environment of peace with a calm mind, you'll reap the reward of peace when you need it.

Nevertheless, you'll also want to begin relinquishing control. Many times, our peace is disturbed by our obsession to command and orchestrate every little thing. Ultimately, you and your ex-husband had enough in common to marry, so there's a particular common ground to help direct your choices concerning the children. Inevitably, certain contrasts in parenting styles will require the release of control on some level. Admit and accept all things are just not going to be *your* way. For those scenarios, there's an essential and profound directive:

Get a Life!

For example, my friend told me that she had anxiety about her ex-husband's plans to take the children to a particular event. She was stirring up trouble about it. More or less, I suggested to her that if she had plans, something fun scheduled, she wouldn't have so much time to scrutinize the kid's activities. She'd be too busy picking an outfit, threading her brows, and getting a bikini wax.

Sometimes the issue is passable and doesn't deserve the attention and chaos we give it. If we have our own things to do, our own interests, hobbies, and life's achievements to attain, we'll have a lot less time to be offended over minor things.

Visualizing Your Way to Power

The goal is to maintain healthy interactions with your ex. So, you're not picking up the phone intending to rip into anyone, even when they deserve it. Before you make a call, relax, and enter into a calm space, emotionally. I want to share one of my many visual exercises that helped me tremendously: I envisioned myself as a queen and envisioned my ex as someone who had no means or status to threaten my sovereignty. I saw myself as whole, abundant, and opulent; therefore, he posed no threat to me. Next, I would breathe – inhaling deeply for five seconds, holding for three seconds, and then exhaling slowly for seven seconds. I would repeat this breath cycle three times. Now you try it. Physically do it, rather than just knowing you should breathe intellectually but making a choice not to practice it in real life. We are moving from simply reading books to actively practicing what the books teach. So, right now…breathe. #whosah

Admittedly as a mother, when your children are involved, it isn't easy to get ahead of your instinct to protect them.

Sometimes proving your determination to heal your family is evident by how you chasten the flesh.

On the one hand and despite there being days when you show up calm and ready to take the high road, there will be times when you're going to lose your mind. *Then* the goal is to reclaim your sanity and your sovereignty as quickly as possible. If you have a heated conversation with your ex-husband about the children, take action to change your state. That conversation put you in fight or flight mode, and now that it's over, it's up to you to let it go and allow your body to release it. A quick way to snap back into wholeness is to take 30 seconds to let out whatever frustrations are brewing. I would sit in my car and let all the anger, frustration, hurt, and disappointment out. I would fuss, cuss, scream, cry, and then take a deep breath. That breath represented me transitioning from fight or flight to homeostasis-I deliberately returned my mind and body to a stable state. I relaxed my brows, my jaw, lowered my shoulders from my ears, and continued to breathe deeply. Changing my breath and my posture caused my state to change. Next, I would verbally speak to myself in what my life coach calls a rant. Then I'd stretch my body to move that energy preventing it from being stuck in my body. Remember, practicing peace involves avoiding unnecessary confrontation, but it also involves knowing how to get back to a peaceful state after everything goes to hell.

If they trashed Jesus & he was known to turn water to wine, gave away free fish platters, healed the blind & had enough power in his hem to heal a woman, then who are you to think you can get people to treat you fairly?

Take some solace in that fact that Mom is Mom. No matter who says what about a mother, the child will always love their mom – it's genetic and innate. Nothing can sever the tie between the child and the mother except for the child and the mother. People jeopardize their relationship with the child when they talk about the child's mother to the child. There's nothing that can split them apart because the mother will be back in tune with the child when he or she returns home. So, sovereign being, when in doubt and enraged by the futile attempts to break you, see them for what they are and adjust your crown. #don'tstoop

Your Son Is Not the Man of the House

I never liked it when people would tell my oldest son Robert he was the man of the house. He was 10 when we divorced, a little boy. I never wanted him to prematurely feel responsible for anything more than his grades, his chores, and his character. Please rethink calling a young boy the "man of the house" in the absence of the father. Remember, the family is in a fight or flight mode because of the shakeup brought on by the divorce. Children are no different, and they, too, are grasping for security, peace, and reassurance. When it comes to a boy being snatched from his childhood to be a man prematurely, there can be an initial novelty, but it may also become a resentment point. Firstly, it's not fair to them, and when you get back to dating and possibly marry again, your son will be dethroned from being "the man of the house"—potentially presenting a built-in contention between your new husband and son. Assure them that it's great to operate in a role as a big brother; take out the trash, make sure the doors are locked, and the alarm set, but that's enough household responsibility.

Communicate that his positive participation with each family member is immeasurable – that his presence is a necessity for the group. But give him a release from filling the shoes of a grown man. I never wanted to curtail Robert's childhood just because my ex-husband was no longer in the home.

Recognizing Pain Bodies

In his book, A New Earth, Eckhart Tolle, talks about how parents pass pain bodies to their children when they are born. He defines a pain body as an "…accumulation of old emotional pain that almost all people carry in their energy field. I see it as a semi-autonomous psychic entity. It consists of negative emotions that were not faced, accepted, and then let go in the moment they arose." Understand, none of this work can be done if we, as women, are frail basket cases or vindictive bitches. I believe children have a voice and inherent questions. Answering their questions could prevent them from cultivating and carrying an active pain-body they could have for the rest of their lives and even passing to the next generation. #yourlegacy

You can help them reconcile some things, in my experience, but if things are too uncomfortable for you, they won't get their questions answered. The more work that you do for yourself, the better you'll be for your children. You owe it to yourself to take the steps and the time to heal and to rejuvenate. Get your coach, get your spiritual counsel, get therapy, and support so you can get clear.

Get everything that you need spiritually and mentally, so you'll be in an optimal space to help manage your children's emotions and take on the heavy-hitting questions they present.

Part 2

Do You Owe Your Children a Happy Mother?

A dear friend told me, "Vivian, you owe *yourself* a happy heart, and your children will immediately benefit from that personal standard. But if you make the mistake of the children being the primary reason you seek a healthy heart, they'll recognize and normalize that imbalance. Do you want them to pick a partner based on that?" Yes, the kids might be why you begin your healing journey, but somewhere along your path to healing, your level of self-love will become a guiding light for you. If you do this solely for the children, you could be inadvertently teaching them to live for other people and care for themselves *after* others' needs have been fulfilled. Despite good intentions, I believe this mindset imparts a curse - the curse of being an unfulfilled shell of a person, a co-dependent zombie.

> More than owing your well-being to anyone, you
> owe your well-being to your purpose.

I remember seeing my grandmother and my mother push through trying circumstances with a forced smile, although they were desperately hurting on the inside. Today we have resources and tools available to us that they never did have. It's up to us to choose to use the resources that are at our fingertips. Imagine how radiant and magnetic you'll be when you're healed, healthy, and whole.

For example, you're a mother, and that's one of many other responsibilities you've taken-on during this lifetime. People are birthed through you as a woman. Brand-new humans spring forth because you are physically able to get them to the planet and emotionally able to love them and care about their growth. You owe it to yourself to maintain your body, reproductive, and general health to facilitate the task of mothering. You will need financial health to support the lifestyle and expenses of the children you bring into the world. And you will need the mental health and emotional intelligence to rear well-adjusted, whole children who are ready for this world system. You give to your children out of the overflow of health you've already cultivated for yourself. Serving your purpose as a mother hinges on your self-care competency, and this dynamic is in play for every other task and mission in your life.

You owe it to yourself to be whole. You being emotionally stable allows you to properly guide your children through the process of doing the same. Consider how your family now has the task of redefining their lives. Your children, your ex, and you are all redefining your roles, standards, and expectations. Your children likely had a world wherein everybody was under one roof, and the family dynamic is now profoundly different and in flux. Each person in the family will need to know how to clarify their needs, desires, and fulfillment levels. They all must do that for themselves but also so they may serve and support the group. Self-care *is* caring for the group. Cultivate this practice in your children by them seeing you cultivate it in yourself.

It's common to see people, especially mothers, obsessively create incentives outside of themselves. Sometimes we find the energy to do something because of an obligation that motivates us to get our stuff together. Sometimes, that will be the best you can do – to leverage the need and expectation of someone else into a reason to go on and keep moving. When possible, we are to first do things for ourselves (think airplane oxygen mask again here). The result will be an inherent blessing to everyone else, but the impetus for this is to be out of a need and desire to continue to have life unfold around us and through us.

Early-on during my divorce, I remember people would ask me how *I* was dealing with things. I would explain to them that I was okay because the children were okay. However, they would emphasize they wanted to verify *I* was personally doing well too. I was so annoyed by that and thought they were a little dense for refusing to accept my initial response. I would put a wall up and wonder why they didn't get what I was trying to say. I scoffed, thinking people who loved their kids would get it. I was stuck on the erroneous notion that knowing that our children were fine is all the comfort a parent needed.

Those people had the wisdom to distinguish between my wellness and the children, and I was the one who had it twisted. They were trying to find a way to share the lesson of self-care with me and were appropriately dissatisfied with my original answer. Truthfully, my assertion that I was okay because the children were okay was a lie.

It was a lie because, by extension, if I wasn't okay, the kids wouldn't be okay. Even if the children managed to be okay independently, I still needed to process everything as a woman, independent of being a mother, ex-wife, business owner, co-worker, daughter, etc.

Just keeping it moving doesn't mean we're okay.

However, we don't want to be too aggressive in our approach when rebounding from a divorce. Being flexible and recognizing when certain concepts are above our spiritual maturity can be liberating. While we endeavor to develop new spiritual muscles over time persistently, we don't want to stress out trying to walk on water too soon. Whatever proves truly therapeutic and whatever gets us to our next level of wholeness holds value in this process.

When matters are desperate, and you need inspiration beyond yourself, let the Creator send whatever and whomever It chooses. Sometimes we leverage other people and things around us to get things going, but ultimately, we have to master our self-care beyond our responsibility to others. Focusing on self-care as a priority is organic, balancing, honest, and emotionally intelligent.

> Eventually, I learned that taking care of me *is* taking care of the kids.

When I take time for self-care, I show my children how to care for themselves even when the sky is falling. They suffer less when I do my emotional housekeeping regularly. I am less likely to fly-off-the-handle or inflict some unnecessary reprimand on them simply because I haven't adequately managed my stress. Some examples of my self-care include yoga, acupuncture, massage, brunch with friends, a sit down for a movie, a private coaching session, receiving Reiki, a solo weekend trip to London just because or to San Diego to pray, meditate and journal on the beach,

Dealing with my issues routinely helps ensure I don't transfer my fears and bitterness to my children.

> Generational curses occur when a previous generation neglects to heal their trauma and imbue those weaknesses in their kids.

In his study of epigenetics, Dr. Bruce Lipton explains how trauma is passed down genetically and how we can heal by going beyond the genes. If the thought is, I'm this way because my mother was this way, then the counter perspective is that I can change my mind and body to be different and start a new pattern to pass down. The final benefit of self-care is the inherent mastery of joy and freedom, also known as being whole! Being whole introduced me to another self-mastery level; I am better at everything I do, notably mothering.

Welcoming His New Woman to the Family

One of my goals was to get to a place where I would vacation together with my kids, my new beau, my ex-husband, and his new love. I wanted my healing to overflow to the family. I wanted the kids to benefit from having all of us in one place and have all of us working together collectively. The adults could take turns having alone time, knowing the children were having fun under adequate supervision.

This blended family/blended vacation idea came out of a scenario that I noticed whenever the kids were doing something with my guy friends and me. I would see the children loosen up and begin to have a good time, but I would inevitably notice Robert's energy shift as if he felt he was betraying his Dad. It was as if he thought he shouldn't fully accept having fun with what essentially appeared to be his Dad's replacement. He didn't feel right about having fun with a man who appeared to be taking his Dad's place in our family. In turn, when the kids would go out to be with their Dad and his girlfriend at the time, they would often act-a-fool because they thought they were betraying me.

So, I told my ex-husband I wanted to meet his girlfriend, and he coordinated it. I tried to get ahead of this thing and find a way to induce the best possible outcomes. At the time, I was a personal trainer, and she asked if I would help her train. We both admitted it was kind of weird but decided not to sweat the small stuff. The rest, as they say, was history! We grew to honor and respect one another, to the point that when things went wrong between my ex-husband and me, she would readily advocate for my side of the argument if it benefitted the kids. It got to be a little funny because my ex-husband would sometimes accuse her of being in cahoots with me. She would side with me so often; he would jokingly wonder if she was on my payroll! Of course, she wasn't; but the truth is I was typically right, so it was easy to side with me.

During that time, I owned that we were a family, a blended family, but a family, nonetheless. We women have so much Divine power; we can call into our family's experience whatever we choose. I didn't know this initially and spent far too much time fighting with him than manifesting over my family. The fighting with him was out of ego and yielded division and calamity. The ego is easily seduced into powerfully going into battle to defend itself. Through coaching, reading, and meditating, I learned to observe and create, not react. So, I prayed for this woman, I called her into our lives, and when I learned they were engaged, I let out a huge sigh of relief, and my heart was full because she's an amazing bonus mom to our children. I know some of you are thinking, "WHAT?!" Listen, I didn't want him on any level, and I knew he would be with a woman. Knowing this, the only thing for me to do is manifest who that woman would be. The woman who would have an impression on my children, I wanted her to be at a level equal to or higher than me, related to character, career, salary, experiences, etc. I manifested exactly what I requested.

Now, this may be too "new age" and perhaps triggering for some, but even the Bible teaches that we are to ask to receive. Ask that your children be connected with a bonus mom, i.e. stepmother, who is whole, centered, loving, empathetic, and nurturing. Ask for someone who is generally knowledgeable about child-rearing and *specifically* gifted for rearing children like your kids.

Write that vision and make it *very* plain – all the things your ex-husband's girlfriend, fiancée, and wife would need to be to bring peace into the situation for everyone concerned.

Knowing what the family scenario looks like in your mind is the predecessor to seeing it with your eyes. Know you are creating this woman, attracting her into your experience, know that she's joining your family. Granted, some women have difficulty imagining their ex-husband with another woman, then you may need to stay married to him if that's the case. If it's possible and advisable concerning safety, and if you don't want to see him with another woman, stay married. For the rest of us, drawing a detailed vision of his new sweetheart is a manifesting strategy, and you'll be surprised by what God sends your way.

When your husband introduces you to the very woman you held in your heart for him, you can smile inside with immense gratitude. You will be face to face with your Divine, co-creative power.

Blended families require a combined effort; everyone has a part, and everyone has a role. Women wield an extraordinary creative power that often goes untapped and uncultivated. Take a breath right here and decide to use the superpower of creative intercessory prayer for our families' good today and, ultimately, for the betterment of our community, society, and the entire world. A tall order, I know. Ask yourself what happens in the world if we let go of old paradigms and contention expectations between divorced family members. Instead, be willing, even eager, to blend the right people into your family so that everyone gets their needs met. What if your quality of life hinges on having the emotional maturity to ask for the right additions to the family and be as welcoming as possible when the new editions arrive?

Now is not the time to distance yourself from the very real changes in your lives. No matter what, your ex-husband will be around, in some capacity, for the rest of your life. The thought that you can pretend he's an old dusty box of memories – that he's a non-factor in your life despite having kids to raise is mean-spirited and delusional.

Real talk, you *are* family, forever!

When you marry and have kids, you create a family and a legacy that's open-ended and ongoing, perhaps never-ending. You and your ex-husband have a litany of milestones to experience with your children. You'll be grandparents together, at weddings together and in a lifetime of experiences for as long as each of your children and their children are alive - therefore, work at making peace with the scenario.

Granted, finding the ex-wife flow takes time. Divorce represents the death of an entity, so grieving is natural. The stages of grief are real and trying to circumvent the grieving process could prove futile. The inherent disappointment the marriage failed has to be processed. You can go on the path of least resistance and get some necessary, professional psychological help to come to terms with things or choose from a litany of other therapies. Acupuncture and regular massages may help move the energy in your body. Still, talk therapy and coaching could help expedite your healing process and may very well be your saving grace. Find someone familiar with divorce and blended families, but don't try to do this alone. "We cannot solve our problems with the same thinking we used when we created them." Albert Einstein.

Try different approaches and modalities until you find what works for you, and then use it persistently, so it continues to move you forward. Don't try to process it alone and without wise counsel. Update and upgrade your vision of family to include the beauty of what's evolving through all of your lives. Be a healthy family; whatever way that plays out for you.

The New Beau

I do not suggest that you try to do this alone.

If there is a man around whose company you enjoy, he could be a shoulder to lean on. Enjoy his company. However, there's no reason to bring children into this if the person is there to help you through a crappy time.

Understand the children are trying to establish a connection with everyone they meet, whether they admit to it or not. Introducing someone and then breaking up with them impacts the kids unnecessarily.

Nevertheless, it's safe to assume that now and then, you'll want to transition from mommy time to grown woman time with someone that provides adult interaction and stimulus. I believe it's crucial to buffer things between that part of your life and your children. Simply, let it be your time and means of self-care.

Again, it does not have to be serious. You may not be dating someone who is family material. It depends on how you met this person and his status and the timing of the divorce. Leave the kids out of it. They don't need to be a party to your dating life. Would you want your ex to introduce the kids to every woman he dates? I'm guessing your answer is no.

Eventually, and after you experience emotional healing and release, you may meet someone and like him. You may even feel you can see him in the fold with the rest of your family. Be sure to hold true to where you are mentally. If you are not healed and still having problems seeing someone with your ex-husband, be cool when deciding to throw someone else in this mix. Any unhealed wounds could manifest as you are attracting a new version of your former man, possibly repeating the very same thing. Spend some time tending to yourself. It could feel bizarre being alone. For me, it was like breaking an addiction to a drug. I realized I was never man-less. I always had a man to text, go out with, spend time with, travel with, etc. So, taking this healing time was not easy, but it allowed me to stop being a boy crazy *girl* and evolve into a *woman* who was appreciative of a man.

Concerning introducing a new serious partner to your ex-husband, I learned I had to let the men be men. Your new man will find his way and his place in your life. I found it helpful to assure my man that there was absolutely nothing between my ex-husband and me. Letting him know your connection is strictly a matter of co-parenting only goes a long way. Reassure him he's your choice, and if he's a straight-up guy, he'll be impressed with the co-parenting life you've created. He'll appreciate how your children are well adjusted and enjoy being introduced into your positive environment.

Side note: By now, you are poised, exuding so much radiant, effervescent energy, don't be surprised if your new man is a tad insecure. After all, he sees a woman who is leading her family gracefully, and this could leave him feeling confused about how your ex-husband "let you go." A little reassurance goes a long way.

It's your place to ensure he understands the co-parenting dynamic and the foundation you've established for your children. This concept is not common in the Black community so understand you're likely exposing him to a new co-parenting paradigm. You're creating the space for him, but it's his responsibility to find his flow in the family dynamic.

If he feels he needs to talk to your ex-husband to establish his place, let the menfolk do what they do. Don't obsess over things or try to control everything.

Be mindful when attempting to advise your new man on how to talk to your old man.

You can lose the new trying to train him to deal with the old. The new beau will compliment what you've already built. You'll know you have the right new man when what he brings to the table fortifies what's already built in your life. You will be amazed at how the Creator can send a perfect match for you and your blended family when you do your part by preparing a life that works and space for the man you're calling forth.

Remember to establish regular opportunities for your children to communicate their thoughts and concerns about any addition to the family. Promote activities and opportunities that allow them to get to know Mister New Man, and please let the children have their feelings. Their feelings are valid, and it feels healthy for them to know their mother is listening to them. Now that doesn't mean they call the shots. My kids were terrible at one point. My daughter Lauren had to be 14 years old when she said she would rally her brothers to act out a scene from the movie, Are We There Yet, starring Ice Cube and Nia Long. I told them, "Ok, I won't date, but Robert, I'll need you to invite me to play your PS3 with you and no other friends, and Lauren, I'll need you to only call me on your cell and talk for hours, not your BFF's from school…ok?" Immediately they said never mind; you can have a new boyfriend. Kids can be just as self-serving as adults; it's a default human behavior. But I laughed because I taught my little crumb snatchers a lesson that day.

Lastly, there is the matter of precaution. While so many men are upstanding, there are those with predatory agendas. Some of these men are often so deep in denial; they don't even see themselves as potential abusers or harmers of women and children.

Vet all newcomers. Period. It's not negative thinking to take precautions. It's no different than sniffing a container of food left in the fridge to determine if it's gone bad and needs to be tossed. Give every potential beau a thorough sniff-test before exposing the children. Generally, children let their guards down when a parent introduces someone, and they tend to trust the people you introduce to them, so be vigilant on their behalf. Remember, as we grow emotionally and spiritually, our intuition is sharpened, and when we are not used to trusting that, we tend to ignore it. NO… TRUST YOUR GUT, EVERYTIME!

Mistakes

From time to time and despite your best efforts, your children may experience some negative things during the divorce and in life in general. I think the best thing to do is have a conversation about things as they happen. Resist the temptation to sweep mistakes under the rug or ignore their effects on the children and family unit.

Consider that a proper conversation
heals a thing.

It will take courage on your part as you exercise keeping your ego in check but going to the child to confess that you could've done something differently can help them heal and help them grow as human beings. The conversation helps immensely because you acknowledge you didn't get something right and that level of transparency induces respect. Apologizing also models the way to live life with integrity and the dignity of self-acceptance. While this is your child's journey, you have so much to do with the quality of their experience. They're going to grow to become adults who will forever reference this time in their life.

Your children's experience with you can be a point of growth, healing, hope, recovery and forgiveness or a place where secrets and resentments began.

Being transparent and talking about things will help your children direct their energy and feelings toward the healing process rather than becoming a victim. Remember, when you deal with things as they come, with honesty and transparency, they can still turn out to be triumphant despite a rocky start.

Look at the Oprah Winfrey's and the Tony Robbins of the world – people who had rough starts in life then went on to dominate the game. There is a way to not only survive but to leverage things to the point of thriving. They still may have their demons and some things for which they may need talk therapy or correction but overall, they are proof that bad experiences don't have to steal our destiny or better yet, perceived bad experiences can be leveraged to shape our destiny.

Convincing Kids You're Innocent

Giving little digs, hints, and comments that your ex-husband was the primary reason for the marriage's failure doesn't help exonerate you. I recall a period where my ex-husband would blame me for stuff, and then I would blame him – back and forth ad nauseam. We would pull the kids into the struggle with unnecessary disclosures of information to prove our innocence. Our son Robert was around 12 when he got fed up and stated that everything was pretty much both our faults. He took the position that our little quarrels should not be presented to him and his siblings at all. He demonstrated more maturity than we did at that moment - teaching us both a lesson in culpability and wisdom.

There is a human need to point at something your ex-husband does and highlight the folly. It's self-justifying, and it's highly satisfying to present yourself as the innocent martyr, leaving him to be the diabolical reason for the sky falling. Considering the thought, someone has to be wrong, and someone has to be right is a misconception. I believe divorce is the result of people changing, and the marriage has served its purpose and is now being transformed. No one has to be the villain, and it doesn't have to be some overly profound moral to the story. However, kids want to know what happened and why things can't stay the same. Because of this, I believe they deserve facts, not stories around the facts.

After we separated, we decided we wanted to have a formal discussion with the kids. We felt we knew enough about what went wrong to guide the children to a broader understanding of how our family dynamic was changing. I also suspected it would settle a few things between my ex and me. I remember telling my ex-husband the kids were far from stupid so let's have a real dialogue with them. I watched an episode of Dr. Phil, and he shared how children handled things better when they are not made to use their imagination about things or kept in the dark.

Dr. Phil advised that it's better to give kids some facts on which to hang their hat.

Most often, children are resilient and mentally capable of handling the truth. It's the lies that destroy them, causing them disease and emotional imbalances. Know the children see through the façade when you claim to be just fine, but then they hear you crying at night or arguing in the next room. They know when mommy and daddy love one another and when they hate one another. Having real conversations and let them know what was going on encouraged more healing and better recovery for our family, literally as a whole.

My ex spoke to the kids and admitted to wrongdoings, and humbly repented. He confessed he messed up and that it tore him up that things would be different for the family by way of divorce. I realize that many parents will not be so transparent.

For those of you who are brave enough to leap, let me share with you that holding hands with my ex-husband to peel back the curtain for our children to see more of our truth was immeasurably freeing for all of us.

EXERCISE 3.3

Affirmations (speak the following):

1. I realize I am going to make mistakes with my kids from time to time and I know we can all recover and be okay as a family.

2. I enlist the help of the Creator and other loving people to help offset mistakes and know the mistakes offer **the lessons** that make us all stronger.

3. I know all of my children's needs do not have to be met through me, so I do not have to be perfect.

EXERCISE 3.4

I know when my children are with their father they are receiving:

Emotional	Physical	Spiritual
1. Encouragement	1. Healthy meals	1. Guidance
2.	2.	2.
3	3	3

Action:

1. Envision your children receiving all of the above while in the care of your ex-husband.

2. Hold that vision while speaking the following: I know when my children are with their father they are receiving: state the items on your list.

Mindset Mastery Exercise

```
┌─────────────────────────────────────┐
│             EXERCISE 3.5             │
└─────────────────────────────────────┘
```

Forgiveness Letters

Formally forgive yourself for choosing your EX by writing yourself a letter.

1) Draft the Letter

    a. Let it Out

        i. Write the words you feel when you think of your ex-husband (use a thesaurus or search the web for synonyms to get a minimum of 20 words on the page).

        ii. Write 5 reasons you married your ex-husband.

        iii. Write 3 reasons you divorced your ex-husband.

    b. Own It

        i. Write 5 reasons why you're not a victim. For example: I ignored signs he wasn't husband material before the marriage.

        ii. Write 2 things you could've done differently.

2) Using the draft and in your handwriting, neatly write out a letter of forgiveness for yourself for choosing your ex-husband.

    Dear (Your Name),

    I felt (words you felt thinking of your ex)…

    I forgive you for (everything you need to let yourself off the hook for).

    You did the best you could with the information you had at the time, and it is ok. Today you realize your power. Today you understand you're absolutely worthy of love because you are love. Love flows to you, through you, from you, and for you. You are more in touch with your feminine power and owning your sovereignty.

3) Burn or shred the letter. Remember, if you're burning the letter, do it outdoors, ideally in your BBQ grill, if you have a charcoal grill. If not, a pot or pan works well; just bring the top to the pot outside with you because paper flies when it's burning, and you don't want to set anything else on fire.

Mindset Mastery Exercise

Four

The Matrix

What is the matrix?
Control.
The matrix is a…dream world built to keep us
under control…in order to change a human being
into…[energy].
—Morpheus (The Matrix film)

O nce we've owned our part in a divorce, even if it's only to admit how we chose our ex-husband as a mate in the first place, we can move into forgiveness and authentic introspection. One of the things that will become apparent is how a matrix of influencers helped inform our choices. We continuously weigh out the expectations of our families, parents, religious order, community, and national culture. We also give a lot of weight to the expectations of our friends and colleagues.

That's a lot of opinions muddying the waters of personal choice and consciousness.

While clearing out feelings of regret and resentment is crucial to the healing process, identifying how you came to make those choices helps to avoid repeating the cycle in the future.

Understand that, by design, influencers are controllers – they exist to establish a specific system of beliefs, even if it means superseding *your* personal will and conviction. Many of these influencers have no ill-intent, and most people are unconsciously obeying their own programming. Regardless of the influencer's motivation, you may find it benefits you to master the technique of discerning, filtering, and getting back to your center. The first step to doing those things begin with recognizing the matrix. Remember, I mentioned Vishen Lakhiani's book earlier in this book? Well, he dives deep into programming and rewriting your belief system. #gethisbook

Movies, TV and Music

No other tool informs your view of gender roles or programs your expectation of what romance looks like more than movies, TV, and music. They're the heavy-weight arsenal in the matrix. Here's a demonstration:

What does the phrase "you complete me" mean?
What does the phrase "you better call Tyrone" mean?
How about "eat the cake Anna Mae" or
"love should have brought you home last night?"

We are full of matrix programming! Interestingly, some of those phrases are on fire within specific communities, while other groups have no frame of reference for the language at all.

Depending on our age group, ethnicity, national, and religious connections, we are touchy and triggered by specific things.

For example, is it rude for a man to ask how much you weigh, your age, or financial standing? At what point in the relationship might he ask about your virginity or sexuality? Is it appropriate to talk about STDs or your number of sexual partners? Should a man always pay for the date, and should a woman know how to cook, clean, and provide the children's primary care? The answers to those questions will vary based on the demographic of the person answering.

We are full of rules and imagery about lovers, full of idioms and buzz words that serve to trigger our behavior and drive our choices in relationships, especially in love. We are also conditioned to behave, sometimes to our peril, within a tiny box created before we were even born.

The media helps to program pink for girls, blue for boys, red for the whore, and the white wedding gown of purity for the virgin bride. How many times has a sparkling image of a white gown programmed a little girl to believe in happily-ever-after marital bliss? How many women are still secretly searching for that handsome prince who will carry her off to share the wealth of his kingdom?

I didn't grow up with very many formal lessons about men and romance. I had my bonus dad and a couple of male cousins who taught me some things, but overall, the matrix of movies, religious influences, books, and media taught me. Admittedly, I tend to gravitate toward cutting-edge thought leaders, and I consider myself more on the autonomous end of the spectrum than your traditional woman. But make no mistake; I was still affected by influencers throughout most of my love-life.

> I didn't get free until I identified my external
> influences about love, purged what I no longer
> needed, and then consciously set new standards
> that reflected my true convictions.

After doing quite a bit of work, my convictions have grown beyond movie images and the subtle rules of engagement demonstrated on TV. The first step in knowing my inner voice was to unplug, doing a media fast – turning off the devices in my life as much as possible. I was amazed at the withdrawal symptoms when I no longer got my dose of alarmist news, sitcom drama, and contrived, superficial romantic tropes. I soon began to question everything and redesign my life according to my values and sensibilities.

Grandma & Mamma Said...

Please consider the previous generations had limitations that are not, at all, for the faint of heart. They grew up during the Depression, World Wars, the Jim Crow era, and times of systemic, blatant misogyny. Those traumas informed their choices and guides most of the advice they give to us.

The family matriarch is significant, and many times serves as the sage and oracle for the bloodline. Even when the matriarch is off the rails with unhealthy behavior, family members often choose to work around her rather than challenge her demands. Add to that an almost mystical sentiment regarding grandmothers, and it becomes obvious why the matriarch's thoughts about family, men, and marriage may easily supersede your convictions about the topic.

The wisdom of the elders is indeed priceless because there is something to be said for life experience and seasoning.

However, I learned to find discreet ways to keep the advice that worked for me and release the rest. Eat the meat and leave the bones – those skeletal remains and vestiges of old standards that no longer serve to elevate our lives in the modern era.

I have heard of women who have married men they never loved or remained married to men who abused and never loved them – all because a mother of the church or matriarch told them it was the best choice to settle. Consider that religious elders may be operating out of a paradigm that made no room for a divorced woman with children. In their day, the nightmare was having to beg on the streets with your kids, so tolerating a cheating husband, as long as he provided food and shelter, was the preferred compromise.

In the same vein, I always suspected the resistance to women making their own money was partly an effort to keep control over women's options. It could be extremely convenient to have a woman stuck at home obeying everyone's orders when she has no means of providing for herself. Understand that Grandma, Auntie, and Momma may give the best advice they have, but it may be born out of an era aimed toward keeping women in line rather than enabling women to enjoy a fulfilled life. We've evolved.

Religion Says...

What does "waiting for my Boaz" mean to you? If you have ever dipped a toe in the full Gospel waters of Christian culture, you would have come across that phrase and the relative sermons that serve to define that expression. Are you familiar with the story of David's lust for Bathsheba or Esther's story and how she leveraged her profound beauty into getting a king to save her people?

> Religious parables saturate our psyche and
> inform much of our beliefs in life and love.

Religion has a lot to do with our expectations of gender roles and trains us to know our place as women. While there are some beneficial, loving tenets in most religions, the problem arises when we assume that the edicts are above scrutiny.

Arguably, religion is the most sophisticated control system known to humanity. Nothing gives people pause as much as the threat of angering God. If God abhors divorce, then you'd better think twice about it. If women are merely helpmates, then they should resist the urge to correct their husbands. If religious text demands obedience, then woe to the woman that challenges any biblical assertion.

For many women, the religious matrix is the most difficult to scrutinize. I believe vetting religious ordinances is a show of honor and respect. It helps to ensure that man-made tradition hasn't been attached to the text, making God's Word and wisdom of no effect or transformative value. No one ran to church more than me when I was trying to heal from divorce so I'm not against religion. However, I learned after a few years of being stuck, the religious doctrines weren't the elixir for my soul's healing. At least not the popular texts taught Sunday after Sunday. They absolutely made me feel good in the moment but by nightfall, I was miserable. I had scriptures to read but no tactile steps or tools to put into practice.

Oprah Says...

Gurus, authors, and public personalities are a blessing to all of us, but none of them, to my knowledge, claim to be a personal oracle to any one individual. We must master the art of filtering information in this age of data overload.

Even the best advice and most phenomenal wisdom can be detrimental if it's taken out of season for your life.

> Understand that even the most inspiring advice
> can be a matrix that lures you away from
> listening to your inner voice.

Everyone runs the risk of not trusting their intuition, making the mistake of waiting to get confirmation from their favorite guru.

Sometimes a thought leader on a talk show – someone who's authored a book or created a workshop-does not address *your* edification. What they advise is real and fantastic, but not for you. Or, they may have part of your puzzle, but their philosophy isn't meant for your family and situation. I'm betting even Oprah takes to heart only the useful advice to her and leaves the rest. Otherwise, she'd be all over the place. This present informational age is an opportunity to master the art of filtering. Meditate to activate your filter.

Society

Society needs you to sacrifice, fight wars for it, pay taxes toward it, and train your children to grow up and provide the same obedient service.

Society is the "they" we always consider when we fear opinions and consequences. We survey the land and see what "they" do and what "they" think about love and marriage. Society has a lot to do with who you chose for a husband, when you decided to divorce and who you'll date and potentially marry in the future. Society is locked and loaded with all manner of rules pertaining to a woman's role, and there's an ever-present threat of ostracization if a woman travels too far out of that box. *They* are always talking, watching, approving, or disapproving.

Society has passed down rules of engagement between men and women for centuries through culture and tradition. We can see it by the idioms that have been programmed into most of us. These expressions serve to scare, minimize, and control us, and they are alive and well in our psyche. Do you recognize any of the following trigger phrases?

Why buy the cow if the milk is free? A woman's
place is in the kitchen. Keep her barefoot and
pregnant. There's nothing like a woman scorned.

Many women believe they are impervious to negative
sentiments about womanhood. Some women believe those things
are old school and obsolete. But I challenge those assumptions.

Each time we refuse ourselves the dignity of challenging
someone's treatment of us, the soundtrack plays in our minds because
we fear being labeled hysterical or, worse yet, an angry Black Woman.

Here's an ah-ha moment: we women are society, too.
Be on the look-out for the ways we inadvertently perpetuate
limiting beliefs about women.

How about we use our power and influence in society to create
new catchphrases reminding women that we are worthy. Worthiness
is our birthright. Worthy of an abundant, peaceful life, worthy of
love, worthy of generous salaries, beautiful homes, loving
relationships, and if you want a husband, it's your right to define how
your partnership will look. All of these desires and thought forms
spring forth from a place of passion, not desperation.

Childhood Trauma Says...

Indeed, we are part of society, part of religious organizations
and family structures that perpetuate controls over one another.
However, let us recognize the most profound influence of all. Many
women have a wounded little girl stuck in their minds – a voice that
rarely stops speaking and rushes to amplify our fears and hang-ups.

Trauma moves when we move, and we run into big trouble when it begins to speak when we speak. The traumas we fail to clear and transcend tend to motivate all our major decisions, devastatingly. When trauma is in control, we do things that make very little sense in a desperate attempt to be okay.

For example, there's nothing like a woman with daddy-issues when it's time to select a husband. What she calls sexual attraction or compatibility can merely be a corrupted understanding of manhood. The alpha male brawn that convinces her that he'll protect her from the world may be the very thing that threatens her overall well-being. The worst part is that friends and family may even see the impending train-wreck, but the woman's childhood trauma convinces her that they are crazy, jealous, judgmental, or deceived.

Not taking others' advice so your own inner voice guides you could prove wise unless that voice is your wounded inner child!

One of my coaching clients shared with me that when she moved out of the family home at eighteen years of age, she felt she had finally survived her childhood trauma. She thought it was time to exhale and sigh in relief because she had made it out of the environment. She later realized she merely ran away from the scene of the crime, but she had not gotten help to heal the scar on her psyche that was left by the assault.

Childhood trauma travels.

When she left home, she took the trauma right along with her. The trauma continued by her own hand through inappropriate relationships with men, detrimental friendships with women that would betray her, poor professional and financial choices, etc.

> While any part of the matrix is debilitating, the
> scars we allow to echo in our minds induce a tormenting
> level of anxiety that can be devastating.

The best way to combat the matrix is to recognize its voice from your own – not your wounded-child voice but that still, small voice— the voice of your Higher Self. You can do this by mapping out your list of values and beliefs, so when making decisions, you'll clearly hear your authentic voice. When you compromise your standards or settle, the voice will challenge you to choose sovereignty despite the myriad of other influences.

Right now is an excellent time to speak to how children are handled in most societies. Personally, I was raised with a family who believed children should be seen and not heard. I forgive them; they didn't have the internet.

> It dawned on me that no one ever formally gives a
> woman the all-clear nod, allowing her to speak and share
> insights and opinions safely.

I believe this creates a woman who always looks for permission to speak and be present in a room.

This chapter's exercise offers an initial set of questions that will help you find your voice and opinion about matters that serve as the driving force behind some of your beliefs. This list will help spark your thoughts on your current beliefs, and from there, you can ask yourself whether or not your current beliefs support you. You may find you no longer believe something you were taught as a child. You may discover you believe something wholeheartedly and feel inspired to shift your behavior to align with your belief. The daily test will be to show up authentically. To make decisions based on your actual views and not based on what the matrix has instilled in you.

Answer each question with the understanding that you get to choose whether to keep the belief or if it's outdated, chuck it, and subscribe to a new idea that resonates with you and aids in you moving towards your goals. For those of us who are parents, construct an age-appropriate list of questions for your children. Pop some popcorn and listen to your children's thoughts and beliefs about essential matters. Try not to program them or dictate to them. Instead, ask them follow-up questions that encourage them to consider all angles of the question or topic in a way that teaches them to use their critical thinking skills.

EXERCISE 4.1

The Matrix Worksheet (establish your belief system)

Questionnaire:

1. Should the man always pay for the date?

2. Is sex a sin outside of marriage?

3. Is "shacking up" (i.e., living with a partner unmarried) a sin?

4. Do you believe being a career woman makes you an absentee mother?

5. Do you expect to have a contentious relationship with your mother-in-law?

6. Do men have a biological need to +have more than one sexual partner?

7. Is it possible for a man to be faithful?

8. Should women dumb-down, to refrain from intimidating men?

9. Should a woman know how to change a tire on a car?

10. Should a woman share her income with her husband or does his money belong to them both, but her money remains her own? If so, why?

11. Should a woman always leave if the husband is unfaithful?

12. Should a man always leave if the wife is unfaithful?

13. Would you date a man with no money and poor credit?

14. Would you marry a man with no money and poor credit?

15. Are you physically attractive?

16. Are you sexy and confident?

17. Do you love yourself? What proves your love for yourself?

18. Is there such a thing as love at first sight?

19. Are most men dogs?

20. Should children be free to ask questions and give opinions about life, divorce, adults, etc.?

21. Is masturbation a sin?

22. Is wearing makeup, wigs & plastic surgery a red flag for self-hatred?

23. Should a man be able to fight and protect the home physically?

24. Should women learn self-defense and learn to save themselves?

25. If a man hits a woman, should she leave him?

26. Do you believe that a man only cries when he's really sorry?

27. Should you tell a friend that you saw her partner compromised, possibly cheating, or do you mind your business? Why?

28. Is there such a thing as happily-ever-after?

29. Is it better to have a broken relationship than to be alone?

30. Would your friends and colleagues respect you if you lost everything?

Mindset Mastery Exercise

Five

Who Am I Without Us?

*"Sister, you know what's right, just do right. You
don't really have to ask anybody. The truth is,
right may not be expedient, it may not be
profitable, but it will satisfy your soul."*
- Maya Angelou

When I became a single mother, I realized my quality of life was entirely in my hands. How could I, a depressed, disappointed, pissed off, fed up shell of a woman, give to my family? How could I start a new with so much emotional clutter? How could I be cooperative when I was left with only the debris from my demolished marriage? I had no idea where to turn, so I went to church. I was there every Sunday for service and again on Wednesday for a midweek pick me up. If there was an evening service on Sunday, I went back for that one too. I fell asleep listening to TD Jakes every night on YouTube and turned on Joyce Meyer as soon as I woke up in the morning. My therapy strategy was soothing at the moment but didn't solve my problem. It was like putting fix a flat on a tire with a slow leak and continuing to drive on it as if it's a perfect tire. Within a few hours, I was flat.

I quickly realized how so much of my self-value
centered on external measurement.
I felt valuable only when I felt validated.

If I got a degree, I was valuable because an educational institution validated my academic talent. If I was married, a man validated my sexual and romantic value as a woman. If I was a mother, I had value because my children needed me. If any of those things diminished or disappeared, I would be back to having little to no value.

This was my life for several years. A dysfunctional nightmare was caused and maintained by me trying to solve a problem with the same level of mind. I needed an elevated consciousness to achieve elevated outcomes. I began reading personal development books and taking courses on refining my mindset to align with the results I desired. I also hired a life coach and joined a community of women who were investing in shifting their paradigm.

Today, my mindset and lifestyle are light years from where they began. Now, I'm in touch with what's genuine for me, above all else. I appreciate every aspect of what I do daily, even on days that stress me the hell out. The fruits of my labor are a direct result of the spiritual work I'm sharing with you in this book. I can finally say I have no regrets; I'm not a victim, nor am I a villain or a hero. I've identified stories that are just that, stories, not truths, and I've cleared my attachment to them. Personal development work has shown me the best use of "lessons learned" is to use it to prepare for tomorrow, not to retell it for support or to sulk and regularly replay what could've been.

I began to self-validate from within and no longer needed outside validation. I re-trained my brain to recognize my deserving based on my being. I am valuable because I'm alive. I reclaimed my right and role as a spiritual being having a human experience.

I know in all things; this too shall pass. Be it good times that I wish would last forever or shitty times that I wish would end immediately. It all passes. That understanding liberated me and strengthened my fortitude- kind of like holding a yoga pose. I'm not too fond of some of the moves in Vinyasa Flow because they are incredibly challenging, but I know it's a flow, meaning give it a couple of seconds, and it'll be over.

The Damage

My ex-husband.

By the time you're curled up on the bathroom floor in a fetal position regularly, you've let things go too long. It's time to triage your situation. There's a moment in time when a woman realizes that reconciliation is not an option, and her greatest fears have arrived. I know what it's like to want to reconcile, to want to fix things in a marriage, wanting to give it one more chance. I also know what it is to be done – outdone, and entirely on the next page. I know what it is to cry in the car between work and home, so the kids don't see the pain. I know about being pregnant and seeing a husband get off a plane with another woman. I've even reduced myself to getting into a physical altercation with a woman over my spouse, and I thank God I didn't end up incarcerated because of that mess.

The post-divorce aftermath may leave you standing over the smoldering ashes of your former life, wondering what the hell happened.

Hold true to the proper perspective as you consider your next steps. For example, losing a home and moving into a rental townhouse because of a divorce may be particularly distressing, but consider that divorce has rendered some women and their children to homeless shelters. It's all relative, so pace yourself as you assess things - and remember material things are replaceable.

The changes were drastic, and I was in denial about how I felt about things. Granted, at the start of a divorce, too many things need to be dealt with, and patching up the small leaks in the boat is not practical. However, post-divorce, it's time to face the truth and clean up the emotional mess and rebuild your identity for you and your children.

Below is a list of some of the negative impacts of divorce. This is not a complete list, nor does this list apply to every woman. It's a list I created based on my personal experience and the experiences of women who've shared their stories with me.

Physical/Health

Hair Loss	Poor Temperament
Acne & Rashes	Incessant Crying
Rage	Anxiety & Addictions
Fatigue	New Ailments/Sickness
Weight Loss/Gain	Depression

Financial

Bad Credit	Bankruptcy
Car Repossession	Borrowing Money
Home Foreclosure	Mounting Debt
Low Grade Groceries	Low Job Performance
Living with Family	

Mindset/Relationship

Bitterness

Spiritual/Religious Crisis

Rift in Family

Self-Doubt & Hatred

This shortlist of circumstances demonstrates the importance of getting ahead of things during and after divorce. The endeavor is not for the faint of heart, but it is critical for the family's wellbeing. This approach helps minimize the debilitating scars as you, your spouse, and your children grieve the death of a marriage. Some scarring is unavoidable, but there is an opportunity for your family to grieve from a healthy place. As a woman, you are an entire Universe; you set the tone for your family's healing; don't minimize your power. Take the necessary time and steps to process your feelings. You never imagined you'd be burying your union, so just as you would grieve the death of a loved one unapologetically, you have permission to grieve your marriage.

I remember feeling like I didn't have the right to grieve my marriage because I decided to get the divorce. In my mind, I thought, "Vivian, you filed for the divorce, and now you're a mess. Just stay married if it hurts so bad to divorce." I didn't know I had permission to want the divorce and grieve the marriage at the same time. This decision to divorce is a big deal, and you deserve to honor your heart and your emotions as you go through this process. Whatever you feel is valid, you aren't crazy; you are hurt. Get help and allow yourself time to feel what you're feeling. For the kids' sake, one or both parents must work to transmute the significant effects of the marriage's failure. What may be surprising is that recovering from a divorce begins with mindset and self-esteem.

Believing in yourself is a vital first step.
Believing you are competent, resourceful, and that you can figure things out and can handle it all.

The next step is to release any obsession with outcomes. One mindset mastery tool is resisting the need to control how things unfold. Let go of attempting to regulate what happens and focus your intentions on being centered even in the most tumultuous storm. Have a short tantrum alone if you must, but instantly get back to the business of trusting the divine order of things. Stand in the knowing that you've planted your seed of intention; therefore, your harvest is imminent.

Have goals and aspirations help you achieve, but release being tied to how it needs to happen and surrender the outcome.

For example, when a woman is pregnant, her role is to provide the best environment possible for the baby in her womb. She can't foretell what the baby will look like, how healthy it will be, or anything else. She's not in control of the outcome, but she can make the small daily decisions that support her baby's health. That's all we can ever do as it relates to our goals. Deepak Chopra calls this the Law of Detachment in his book the 7 Spiritual Laws of Success.

Have a desire, take actions that support the manifestation of the desire but allow things to unfold as you stay present. Always having something to look forward to is inspiring, but there is so much power in being present and staying in the moment. Holding on to an outcome can rob you of the present moment fulfillment. When I'm present with my children, our discussions feel more connected, and they know I see them, I hear them, and they're essential. When I'm outcome-driven, they sense that as well, and it doesn't feel as fluid.

Regretting what happened yesterday doesn't help today.

I believe it's natural to reflect on our lives and evaluate where we did well and where we missed the mark, but it can be counter-productive when that look back results in regret. I am thinking of Mary J. Blige's lyrics about eleven years of sacrifice with nothing to show. Many women berate themselves for making decisions that did not pan out ultimately.

I want to offer you a perspective shift. Consider that you fulfilled precisely what you needed, and your ex-husband allowed you the opportunity to do that. So now that the marriage is over, it's easy to put your entire marriage in the failed category negating the good because it didn't work, but please don't do this. There is beauty in your story, although it didn't unfold as you desired.

I knew from the beginning my ex-husband didn't want what I envisioned. He wasn't *that* guy, and he told me from day one. So many times, our regret is a result of trying to force something to be something it's not.

My advice is this: don't regret anything. Learn the lesson, so you prevent a reoccurrence.

Also, many of us women spend so much energy manipulating men that when he breaks through and makes his own choices, we feel betrayed. I've been there – wanting my ex to be who I needed him to be, regardless of his purpose or desire. For example, I prefer older guys; some say it's because I didn't grow up with a father. I say it's because I respect intelligence, wisdom, calmness, and a mature perspective. I don't like immaturity, foolishness, or men looking to me for the answers, so when I encounter a man with insight, I enjoy the wealth of knowledge and bask in it. I was attracted to my ex-husband because he represented freedom. I wanted to be free from what was expected. I grew up attending church two to three times a week and twice on Sunday. I was in Sunday school, bible class, and prayer meetings weekly. When I was a teenager, my mother finally allowed me to sing in the choir, so add in another church attendance for choir rehearsal. My ex, however, was very street-savvy, and I was attracted to and mesmerized by his swag. He was eight years older than me, and that added a protective component that was alluring.

These things were triggers from traumas I picked up long before I met my ex, but since I hadn't done the work to heal, I brought the trauma with me into my relationship. Actually, my trauma did the choosing.

When I filed for divorce over a decade later, it wasn't due to any new information about my ex. I knew his philosophy on relationships from day one.

He hadn't changed much, but I changed enough to face the truth that I was the one ignoring the signs and proceeding to try to make him dance to my tune in hopes of changing him for my purposes. Now, the challenge was not to be mad at myself, knowing that I did the best I could with the information I had at the time. By many accounts, he fulfilled in me what I needed to be fulfilled.

It's funny because before I married my ex, I dated a man who was the equivalent to the Carlton character from the TV series *Fresh Prince of Bel-Air,* asking for my hand in marriage. He offered all of the security in the world, but I chose my ex – the one who didn't want to be a husband. The brokenness that I'd encountered due to choosing my ex-husband despite having another man offering honor and fidelity was a manifestation of what I believed I deserved deep down in my psyche. I was attracted to the man that, at the start, confessed that he was going to see other women and that he didn't want me seeing anyone else. I convinced myself that he didn't mean it and that he would stop that craziness when we married. I thought his statement about seeing other women would evolve, but it was really a firm declaration.

Ultimately, I've never dated a guy who surprised me with his behavior. They all showed me who they were very early on, but I chose to ignore the red flags because it was more important to me to be with them than to not be. As I talk to women, they tell me they also dated the illusion they created in their mind, not the man in front of them. Many of the women I meet through my coaching business admit that their ex did not pull a fast one, changing into someone completely different than the guy he was during courtship. When I ask them to name some positive things about their ex, they rattle off some things, but it tends to be basic attributes that don't facilitate lasting relationships. I noticed a lot of our sisters enjoy being Nurse Betty.

They hope to bond themselves to a man by rescuing him. Women try to sculpt a work-of-art out of a man, but he isn't showing up in our life as clay to be molded. He is already a finished work of art, and it's a waste of time, energy, and effort to try to play as if we're his god. Since fixing him is the absolute wrong approach, why not pass on those that don't fit our life and continue to date until we encounter the one who shows up a whole man who fits?

But here's the rub, we can only attract who we are and where we are – so the sculpting we try to do on the men in our life is better served when it's the work we do on ourselves.

It may be time to face the fact that your marriage wasn't an example of you being abandoned or misused, but an example of you not doing the work in your own heart and mind to make more authentic choices and attract healthier prospects. Question: Did your trauma pick your husband?

The great news is that you have value in and of yourself, without validating a husband or a career. You have value standing on your own and have nothing to prove. Conversely, you are a co-creator in your life, and every choice you make reflects the spiritual power and maturity you've cultivated. You don't ever have to convince anyone that you're worthy, but you inevitably confirm what you believe you're worth by the choices you make.

What Role Do Women Play?

I think gender roles have been entirely obliterated over the last two decades. Things are not the way they formerly were and are ever evolving. We have the internet, stay-at-home dads, and new social standards that yield new options for everyone – male and female.

Moreover, since an increasing number of women generate revenue and no longer need a man's income for food and shelter, we are free to love a man without necessitating him to be our refuge. There's a power of attraction guru, Esther Hicks, who promotes a low-pressure revision to the modern-day marriage vow with the following, "I like you pretty good, let's see where it goes." While that's a bit too liberal for most, it does convey the idea that it's a marriage at will, so no pledge of 'til death do us part'. But a mutual agreement made by two whole individuals who've taken ownership of their happiness.

> When a man isn't the center of the woman's universe,
> he no longer leverages a woman's need for him to
> manipulate her into tolerating disrespectful
> and non-desirable behavior.

Thus, when a woman takes the stance that she doesn't hold a man responsible for how she feels, she inherently encourages him to pursue his real interest with more transparency. Since we attract who we are, not what we want, who we attract, will allow us to see where we are. This awareness serves as a true north for women desiring to be true to herself and authentic in her dealings. When we find ourselves caught up with the wrong guy - The next move is the one that sets the tone for how you unfold within the relationship. Do you end it, or do you compromise and make excuses for why you should stay and see how it develops? If both partners are transparent and not operating from lack, there will be no deception.

Going into a marriage to join somebody and help them do their soul work in life is a big responsibility. However, traditional American culture approached marriage from a limited "you complete me" perspective. It wasn't about spiritual growth, but more about an early, redacted version of the relationship. It was as if our spouse would be there to help create this family that, in turn, would somehow guarantee our fulfillment. The idea that marriage and family will be our saving grace is misleading, especially now that we aren't dependent on each other for financial support. A far more promising approach is to pursue relationships from the viewpoint of thoroughly enjoying another person's spirit and energy and allowing that to birth ideas and inspirations to create and share as a partnership/couple.

> I believe everyone is on the planet for their own journey, and if you happen to find someone with whom to partner, it's not for you to claim their journey for yourself or give yours away.

Ultimately, modern-day gender roles are embracing more transparency and autonomy.

Many women are losing tolerance for being treated like children or being defined by outside entities. This sentiment is evident in the innovation of terms like "mansplaining". The pejorative term speaks to the longtime tradition of seeing women as infantile and oblivious. As if women need a condescending explanation, similar to the one you'd give a kindergartener.

Also mentionable is the ever-present backlash to all of the changes. While the rules of gender are evolving, there is a concerted push to return to the old rules and traditions – a time when women suffered more quietly, knowing their place. Feminism is a very dirty word in many households, as its tendency to break from patriarchal tradition is off-putting for some people. However, it's up to each of us as a woman to decide how we will present our gender expression to the world. Each woman deserves to keep the part of traditional gender roles that work for her and suspend without any obligation to uphold man's antiquated traditions.

What the System Taught Us

. . . .

In the past, gender roles helped society control the narrative. Women were taught to be one thing and men another. When a person didn't fit into the gender box, they risked ostracization. Today with more autonomy, men and women honor their internal interests and beliefs without checking-in with social norms or looking for permission. But there remains a stigma to a woman exploring options.

Overall, I believe women are discouraged from celebrating their worth and opportunities for reasons of control. Society trains men and women for different roles, but let us not forget, society tends to indoctrinate each of us into servitude to it and only in the last few decades, superficially serve ourselves. Slavery is a perfect demonstration of the dynamic.

Society, through the members of the ruling power, conspired to harvest the worth and value of an entire group of people for society's progress and at the expressed detriment to the individuals of that population. The apparent first offense is heinous enough, but tragically, society's progress also meant the loss of culture for the enslaved.

What our ancestors discovered, practiced, and passed down for generations, our truths, were forbidden. The knowledge and wisdom maintained for thousands of years because it efficiently served the collective were suddenly risky to practice. There never was a point in which the original values were restored. How could it be? How do women and men teach their daughters the superior traditions of her tribe that worked effectively for them as a people when they don't know them? Especially since slavery reduced a black woman's worth to physical labor, sexual, reproductive, and domestic purposes under deplorable conditions, with brutality and without apology and restoration. How can gender roles and tradition be upgraded and repaired for a terrorized, decimated group of women?

My friend told me about an emotionally disturbing scene in Halle Berry's film, Queen. Her character was passing for white and had a white suitor who was smitten. Queen decided to tell him about her African American heritage, and his brain appeared to switch to the alternative rulebook set aside for Black women during that time. Enraged, he sexually assaults and berates her, saying she got what all the women of her kind deserved to get. The film is based on a true story, and it begs the answer to the question: what informed his belief that Black women "deserved" rape and abuse, but not White women?

The same thing is in play with Black men, as they were reduced to serving as laborers and breeders only - animals, not human beings. They were murdered, beaten, taunted, terrorized, and had no dignity or respect. How do women and men teach their sons the superior traditions of their tribe that worked effectively for them as a people?

How would any generation ever get the *all-clear signal* to return to the dignity of their elders' former status in tribes; medicine men and women, carpenters, electricians, great hunters, cooks, scientists, griots & leaders?

That all-clear signal must come from within the individual and, subsequently, the collective. Society has too much riding on a collective's lack of self-worth and tribal tradition. Regarding women, especially Black women, society benefits considerably when a Divine Goddess is diminished to a downcast, pious, indentured servant. Society benefits when the Black man hates himself and Black women-this is the house divided. The rampant disregard of Black lives is blatant as murderous police are not brought to justice for brutally killing Black men and women. Society has been effective at protecting what feeds its system by the continued exploitation of Black men and women.

Dr. Joy DeGruy, a Psychologist, Social Worker, and renowned Racial Historian, argues that the psychological scars of the Black Holocaust would inherently be seen in the way that men and women interact with one another and present themselves to the world.

She argues that if military men and women return home with varying degrees of PTSD as a result of fighting wars for years, and if their children and family who did not serve in wars, present certain anxieties and conditions as a result of being raised and domiciled with a PTSD suffering family member, then why wouldn't there be marked residual effects to the African American experience?

Surely, parents who have been stabbed, beaten, raped, sodomized, robbed, burned, hung, and exploited for generations would inherently present with a cornucopia of mental distress. Their children's children would be subject to that neurosis in accordance with the PTSD-like distress of the rearing generation. Add to that the internal and external violence and sexual molestation of both men and women, and you may realize the dire need to question everything. I began to think about what societal conditioning taught me about womanhood. What system defined the rules of being a good woman? I realized it was the same system responsible for the Black Holocaust, both centuries ago and today. #blacklivesmatter

I also considered what system taught my ex-husband how to be a man.

Realizing the effects of history and the loss of culture helped to soften my heart toward my ex-husband enough for a tiny seed of forgiveness to grow. Who would need ego-stroking more than the sons of the line of men that have been so thoroughly disparaged? Who would be more out of touch with their creative sexual power and dignity than Black women when our sexuality had been so cruelly perverted and exploited? We're being called to do the work. To awaken, to become curious and solution centered and to be open to healing our traumas. There's too much riding on us staying asleep and remaining oblivious about our abilities and our worth. Society is not likely to have a coming-to-Jesus moment to treat us more honorably. As Black women, we're being called to heal. As we heal, our men heal. As our sons and daughters witness us operate from a space of wholeness with their fathers, they learn how to be a woman and how to treat a man. As we do the work as an ex-wife to become whole, complete, and needing "no thing", we demonstrate a Divine Goddess energy in our interactions with their fathers.

> You're raising the bar and setting a standard
> for your family. Your ex will rise, or he'll
> be extremely uncomfortable being a
> fool all by himself.

Arguably, we cannot trust our definition of romance and true love until we identify the origin and intent of the traditions that informed our beliefs.

The filmmaking industry presents a good analogy. During the filmmaking, camera operators program the color white into specific cameras. The process is called "white balancing." The camera tech points the camera toward something white on the set, and the camera references white as a baseline to determine the other colors in the room. If the standard white is true, the camera will interpret the other colors accurately. This is a perfect analogy to the importance of questioning traditions, religious edicts, and family customs.

Sometimes what we've been taught sets a false baseline in our lives, and that sets an erroneous standard for everything else – especially concerning gender, love, and marriage.

Body Shaming

I've always been thin in size. As a kid, I wanted to stay with my Aunt Stella in Saginaw during the summers because she cooked a lot of peas and I'd heard that eating peas would give me curves. I thought I could return to school after the summer, and I wouldn't be made fun of for being skinny.

But it never worked. I always returned from Saginaw to Detroit, still skinny. When I tried and failed to gain weight in my twenties, I decided my size zero frame was beautiful despite the fuss in my culture over the fuller figure. After giving birth to 3 children and returning to a size 0, I realized that I would never have curvy hips and a big butt. For years this made me feel less than and inadequate. Curvy women would often comment about how the wind will blow my 'little ass' away. I remember walking into a basketball game with my date, and this woman told my date, 'man you better feed her.' Yes, culturally, I did not measure up and was not worthy of a man because Black men like hips and ass. Sir Mix A Lot solidified that with his hit, *Baby Got Back*. I believed there'd be men who would love what I offered and how I was packaged, and over time, I realized that the more I loved my complete self, body and all, the more I attracted men who echoed my sentiment.

When my daughter was 13 years old, her naturally inherited petit frame caused her to deal with the same ridicule from school kids. I had dealt with my issues in a way that saved my daughter from carrying that cross. I taught her how to manage the ridicule. I was happy to be there for my daughter on the issue. I realize that this demonstrates the importance of overcoming our hang-ups and to not pass them on to our kids. If I had not healed myself regarding the matter, I would have been a source of pain for my daughter.

I would have confirmed her fear that she wasn't
good enough – that she needed to eat more peas to try
to have a fat ass so she'd be attractive.

The Power of Sex

I wasn't taught to face and manage my sexuality, and I don't know a woman who was. We all get a conversation about our monthly period, but no discussion about the beauty and acceptability of our sexual urges and desires. Our sexuality is not dirty, immoral, or evil, but society or rather, the patriarchy has sent a clear message of what makes a woman a good woman and what makes her a whore.

A woman rooted in her divinity is in command of her sexual power and freely embraces it as a tool to give and receive. Empowered women understand the power they possess and don't shrink to using sex in a desperate attempt to "put it on him" or to make a man fall in love, which is highly unlikely, by the way. Disempowered women fail to realize sex is their option to exercise because they want to experience an orgasm and fulfill intimate urges. I repeatedly hear women say they've never had an orgasm through penetration and that they don't feel comfortable telling a man how to touch their bodies to enhance their pleasure.

I remember feeling excited because the man came/climaxed. I thought, giving him an orgasm endeared him to me. I hear women echo this same sentiment often. The theory that making him cum will help ensure he'll keep her around. She even feels as if she's controlling him to a degree. "I made him cum; he couldn't hold it" is a high five moment.

Conversely, when he doesn't have an orgasm, we feel something is wrong with us. Often women are taught to believe that sex is expected and submitting to it is how a woman gets or keeps a man. Women bond with sex, men don't, and after seeing so many fail at using sex as a bonding agent, why haven't we updated our mindset around this?

I believe authentic bonding starts with self-love. Know thyself and love thyself. What does it look like to love yourself? My journey to self-love was layered and complex. I didn't recognize how much self-hate disguised itself as self-love. I peeled back the layers of unworthiness that were disguised as sexual prowess. I peeled back the layers of insecurity that were disguised as loyalty. I peeled back the layers of inadequacy that were disguised as over-achieving. I remember dating this man, and he would tell me he was late for work in the morning so that he couldn't make his lunch. Well, I would whip up something delicious and drop it off at his job on my way to work.

Hindsight, he wasn't deserving of me coming to the rescue for his lunch. He didn't even express gratitude, but my fear of not measuring up drove me to thaw out some chicken breast at 7 am, season them up, and put them in the oven. At the same time, I showered and got three kids ready for school, then popped back in the kitchen to cook. I whipped up broccoli or spinach, rice or potatoes, hot water cornbread, or crescents, all neatly packed and ready for delivery. I'd fly out the door getting everybody to school, just in time to drop off his lunch and make it to work without being late. He was not deserving of this on any level. Looking back, I can identify several occasions where I didn't exercise self-love. I didn't know how. I thought self-love was getting my hair and nails done regularly. I felt self-love was getting an occasional massage.

It was a process of unlearning and remembering. Now I'm at a place where I love myself on a cellular level. One example of cellular level love for me is I love my menstrual cycle. I don't fear it. I don't hate it. It's not an inconvenience; it's my body operating at its peak state, releasing what no longer serves me. Yes, my cycle alters my daily routine, but now that I accept my cycle, changing my routine isn't an inconvenience. It's a reminder to slow down; I feel it's an honor, and it's a sacred time. As I embraced my sexuality, including my sexual organs, I was introduced to tantra and kundalini. The deeper I went within, the more I learned about the amazingly complex being that is me. I was so captivated by the mystery of Vivian. I no longer felt the seduction of being intertwined with a man at any cost. There was nothing more fascinating to me than me. It was a process of getting to know myself on an intimate level, and I wondered how we could make this a rite of passage for girls? We called our period 'the curse' and hated it when it was our time of the month. I didn't embrace my period until I was 46 years old. I agonized over my period for over 30 years. Now that I am nearing menopause, it's ironic that I'm at a place where I value the process of being on my period.

Getting reacquainted with your authentic self is a demonstration of self-love. In my experience, when I'm in love with myself, mind, body, spirit, and womb, it's contagious; I attract that same love from others.

Stop counting on sex as a bonding agent, and please don't think a baby helps procure a commitment.

I don't remember hearing an empowering conversation about sex until I talked with my daughter. Our talk wasn't about shaming her for having biological needs and basic human curiosity but instead conveying her power as a woman. Although sex can't make a man do something, and it doesn't wield all power, sex does carry an energetic, procreative force that's all its own.

I remember telling my daughter that sex is a beautiful thing and extremely enjoyable.

However, it's wise for a woman to consider the reason she's having sex. We are mammals and animalistic. We may see something, smell a scent, kiss too long and suddenly awaken that fire. I shared with my daughter that it might start with someone hugging you; you'll be ok at first, but something could happen, and all of a sudden, you may become aroused. If you don't want to have sex, it's in your best interest to stop the train before it picks up momentum. There's a small window of opportunity to stay ahead of the reproductive impulse. Before thousands of years of biology wins the war over your left-brain senses, release that hug and change the scenery.

It's often animalistic, so as a woman, it's up to us to be intentional with how far we let things go. Those conversations enabled my daughter to go through life without labeling sex as wicked.

I heard someone say, don't have sex with anyone who you wouldn't want to be, and I've echoed that in many social groups. Women have a womb and when we allow access, whoever enters our bodies leaves a part of themselves in us, with us, regardless of whether they are wearing a condom. Energetically, you're tied to him. For more on healing your womb, check out best-selling author Queen Afua's book, Sacred Woman: A Guide to Healing the Feminine Body, Mind, and Spirit. Follow her on Instagram and find her on YouTube to hear her talks on the sacred woman and womb care.

The thing with becoming reproductively mature is that society's hang-up with sex inadvertently creates the problems and negative experience attached to it.

Society's unwillingness to release the stigma attached to female sexuality causes women to be deceptive about their impulses and to approach the topic as though they were infantile. As we heal sexually, we become empowered and break the generational curse; giving our daughters space to make choices based on information and not fear or shame.

A young woman develops this feminine form and doesn't know what to do when a man approaches her. In contrast, he has practiced what to say many times and has been schooled by other men on the art of seduction. Sometimes a man approaches a young woman with very little care about his impact on her life, but he's put every thought into convincing her he's the one so he can *fuck* her.

> **When the right man says the right thing, a woman surprises herself with her sexual response because she likely didn't become aware of her sexuality until she was asked to act on it.**

She's not a whore, and she's a lot less irresponsible than her unplanned pregnancy may suggest. This likely happens because she, like so many other women, was raised to tip-toe around her sexual curiosity, and as a result, got caught up in it without mastery of it.

With sex, it behooves us to be prepared before the opportunity arises. If chastity is the goal, I would first ask why? If it's because you value yourself and have a standard by which you live, excellent! You've got this under control. But if it's because you intend to manipulate and use sex as leverage, then keep yourself out of compromising positions. Biology is a hard animal to train, but it's a lot easier to get out of a situation if you've healed and are clear on your sexual intimacy standards. If he's not the one, his words and touches may not have an arousing impact; they may even turn you off. Self-love helps you to operate from a sane space and not seduced superficially.

In many cases, men are naturally attracted to women and want to have sex with us; it's as natural as the birds and the bees. It serves a woman to be aware of her power to direct and/or redirect that energy. Redirect example; a man asks you out to dinner. You know you want a lighter mood but don't want to deflect his advances nor be tempted; counter his dinner offer with an invitation to lunch, brunch, or coffee instead. Daytime is less sexual – Music artist Whodini coined the phrase with their song, *The Freaks Come Out at Night*.

Consider that a broken man is an
outward manifestation of a
broken woman & vice versa.

When your connection to your sexuality is broken, you may be more likely to attract men who are also sexually broken – men who misuse sex as proof of manhood. Thus, it benefits us as women to establish our sexuality, standards, and interests. It's essential to heal from past mistakes, forgive, and learn lessons. By all means, do not suppress or ignore your sexual desires and curiosities. Be brave enough to be authentic and vigilant enough to keep it sacred.

EXERCISE 5.1

Affirmations

1. I am whole and complete.

2. I am excited & appreciative that I am discovering my own identity, value, talents, interests & power for myself.

3. I make healthy choices that support my vibrance and vitality.

4. I appreciate how my regard for my body is beginning to increase.

5. I feel more & more energy & inspiration every day.

6. My job & living situation are supporting my ability to rebound & get to my next level.

7. I am a woman whose family is healing, learning to manage our emotions, forgive and come together.

8. I believe in myself & my ability to raise my children, to co-parent with my ex and to live my highest purpose.

9. I am in touch with my Divine feminine power and I'm excited to learn more about me.

10. I love, celebrate and appreciate my body.

Six

Moving Forward

"The truth is, unless you let go, unless you forgive yourself, unless you forgive the situation, unless you realize that the situation is over, you cannot move forward."
—Steve Maraboli

I t's time to go for the gold! After we've done the work to free ourselves from the social programming that misinformed our choices, and when we've forgiven ourselves for the decisions that brought pain and divorce, we're ready. When we've released our ex-husband and created a lifestyle that yields a foundation for our children's best life and cultivated a co-parenting haven that works better than some marriages, it's time to go for the home run!

Creating a desirable lifestyle for the next chapter of your life takes strategy and accountability. Gone are the days when we assume things will happen organically, without focus. You will want to master some level of your Divine feminine to create the life you deserve, and you'll do this with the same tools used by billionaires, sages and mentors, media moguls, religious icons, and the like.

One of the first components is knowing who you are and being clear about how you present to the world.

Who You Are

Some of us go from living with our parents to living with our husbands with very little time to map out who we are, individually. We go from being someone's child to a college student, to a wife and mother, community leader, PTA member, etc. We often do this before we understand our power and personality as a co-creator. At what point do we as women consider what type of women we are, what values we have, preferences, and pet peeves?

Are you the type of woman that wants to be financially supported by a husband? Do you want your husband to keep you safe and protected, or do you believe that, as an adult, you are primarily responsible for your prosperity and personal welfare? Do you even want a husband? Are you interested in being a wife?

The next chapter in life requires us to know what we want from ourselves, from a man, a job, friends, and family interaction. Having this understanding is vital to avoid aligning ourselves with people who have philosophical differences - things that will stir-up contention and ultimately heartbreak. When we don't know who we are, we're just sampling everything. We're not intentional.

> When we're focused on experiencing wealth, health,
> and opulence for ourselves, we gravitate to
> people and opportunities where that manifests.

It's like refusing to shop at the discount, low-quality shoe store when you know that quality, healthy footwear is a firm standard in your life. We limit or refuse to frequent fast-food restaurants because we have a new standard of wellness and know they don't provide the product that supports that effort. What are your standards? An exercise that helped me was to list 25 things that I brought to the table.

The world will fill-up that list of 25 things with its own agenda if you don't firmly establish those things on your own.

What do you like? What's your love language?

For example, I enjoy my man coming in from work or the gym, sitting beside me, and laying his head in my lap. I like positioning myself to be ready to receive him. Showered, food prepared, and eager to connect. These things are valuable to me, and I position myself for the experiences that I desire. When I expect him home, I'm spring-fresh, sitting in a place where he can come in, sit beside me and lay his head on me. No, not all the time, but this is what I like to experience frequently. People are naturally busy these days; calendars are full, but I carve out time for moments like this, and my partner looks forward to it.

I understand some men may not like this. One of my things is that he needs to nestle into me as I rub his face and head. I know what turns me on and being clear and at peace with it helps ensure I attract the type of men who stands in agreement with it.

Another example of my established preference is I like to be doted over; yes, make a fuss over me! I've decided that's my standard. I'm a big deal and worth being doted over. I've had men tell me, "your money is no good here, you just keep doing what you do." They valued what I gave and hungered for something as simple as scalp massage, youthful energy, and sometimes a complete overhaul of their client management system. Yep, I'm techy. Suppose he's not using the latest, most efficient apps to manage his real estate, client logs, scheduling, and invoicing. In that case, I'm migrating data to new systems, setting up integrations, and our pillow talk will be how to use the new system. I also love to dance, workout outdoors, pop in a yoga class here and there, and hit some golf balls when I can, and I create dates for us to do these things together. I am crystal clear on what I bring to the table, and I'm equally clear about who I want to attract. The men I attract put a premium on what's included in my package. By the time you finish this book, you'll be crystal clear on what you bring to the table and who you want to sit at your table too!

It's unattractive and unfulfilling to go through life as a woman who doesn't care enough to know what she wants because she's too busy figuring out what her man wants and spends all her effort trying to squeeze into that mold.

This book is your ah-ha moment, your divine nudge to write the script for your life. You are the director, producer, and art designer of your movie. None of the things that happen in your movie occur organically. There's a network of folks ensuring that the desired action happens on cue. Indeed, our lives are like a stage play. We've got to set the scene and the tone well ahead of receiving the actors to act and then let the magic happen with a little light and ambiance.

Now calling the shots is the masculine, authoritarian side of your personality. Most of us flip flop between the masculine and feminine all day. However, if you want a masculine man, he's attracted to the feminine. Take time to study feminine energy principles and practices to be clear on what you're emitting at any giving time. This study will also help you learn ways to increase your feminine magnetism.

Be receptive!

Men need to be received - it's literally a part of the structure and design of their form and bodies. Receive your suitor – his gifts, his time, and his gestures with kindness. The feminine is intuitive and ready to respond appropriately. Know how you want to give your love to your man and know-how to receive his in return.

I notice that men poke out their chest when they do something helpful, and I let them know that they did a great job. Men love to know they have a place in your life and provide value to you as a woman. For example, intellectually, some men not only keep up with me but teach me more than a few things. I know being with the man who falls behind is never a real option because there are so many other men who are up to snuff. Know the man's caliber and be ok to say no to those who aren't a match.

It's essential to know what you want. You don't have to express it to the man but recognize for yourself and if it becomes a conversation by all means with grace and ease, let it flow from your lips. If you present who you are and it's off-putting to a dating candidate, it's just not a match. This doesn't have to mean it's something wrong with either person. If you suffer from a chronic sense of lack and desperation, you could have a hard time letting *Mr. Wrong* walk away.

Authenticity attracts authenticity and repels bullshit.
Believe you're worthy, flaws and all, and he will agree.

There's also something to be said for adequately conditioning a man. Men love it when I show them appreciation for doing things that turn me on. When he opens the car door for me, I do a little shoulder shimmy, give him a girlish grin, and look up at him to fasten my seatbelt for me. After my seatbelt clicks, I hold his face next to mine and kiss him, which gets him every time. Another one of my enchanting moves is the stroking of his head and neck when I return from the powder room in a restaurant. Oh, and when he catches me gazing at him from across the room as if my eyes are saying come back to me, that gets him every time.

Acknowledge his attention to detail and commend him on his ability to give you pleasure. Master feminine ways and encourage the behavior that you appreciate. I've had men tell me they love how kind I am to servers at restaurants, the valet, the grocery deliverer, and the like. They say they've dated women who are rude to servers, and that was a turn-off. How you treat others is a viable demonstration of who you are as a person.

Who He Is

If you have a man whose core values align with yours and he's good at the 3 out of 5 things that matter to you, then let your heart and spirit lead you. But if you are dealing with someone who has very little redeeming quality and trying to play dumb, ask yourself, "Why?" Is your trauma doing the choosing? Is this a call for self-love? Once you know who you are and figure out your role - what you bring to the table, it is easier to say yes to what resonates and no to what doesn't. That evolution will become a standard, and it will bless your life.

A quick note about venting to your girls: Your girlfriends can have the best of intentions, but when you fill their minds with stories about your beau, you're inviting foreign energy into the mix. Although it is a cultural tradition, venting to your girls about your man is counterproductive at best and sabotaging at its worse. If there is a conversation you want to have because there's something you want to see him do differently and you need external support regarding the matter, seek wise counsel, not the high-five gang. My rule of thumb when I need advice is to ask men about men. Formerly, I consulted with my friends, but everyone is speaking from their reference frame, which didn't prove to be wise or beneficial. Men give the best advice about men.

I only consult women that are killing it
in the relationship game.

Our everyday girlfriends can't fix our relationship problems. They don't know what to do, and any advice they give you is just a guess. The play by play of your negative experiences brings down the group's energy and vibe and creates a bias against your man. I used to hash and rehash things with girlfriends for hours, and it was a ridiculous cycle.

The only person that could genuinely add substantial value was my partner. Keep everyone else out of it and solve your challenges with your man. You vent with the girls, and then your man is judged on private matters. He walks around while your friends know things about him that they shouldn't. That's disrespectful, and in a sense, you've betrayed him. Hold items in confidence about your sweetheart, train your ego to find its validation without sacrificing the trust between you and your man.

Be careful with feeling entitled to vent in the first place. While it's a popular practice, I'm not convinced of the benefits, and arguably the sounding board doesn't fix anything.

> When I need to throw a tantrum, I do that in private,
> by myself, and I limit the time on that.

In relationships, we hold space for the other person's growth and healing. While we stand firm in the core objectives, we also temper and balance that with mercy. We are not perfect as women, and our men have to forgive and make allowances for us as well. So being kind and thrifty with your words could prove to be advantageous.

About the Divorce...

How do you approach the subject of your divorce to family, employers, friends, and dating candidates? When you are first getting divorced, you may want to refuse comment for a measure of time. Divorce is a very delicate, precarious space, and you're likely very foggy about certain things. During my divorce, I didn't get into details. I moved to another state and pretty much told one girlfriend, primarily because she assisted the move. If things are happening around a holiday, you may want to smile for the camera during festivities until the divorce logistics are in place. You have the option of making a formal statement to your inner circle and family but being sure to grant yourself the personal choice to go radio silent about all or parts of it.

As for affording your employer (direct manager) some disclosure about the divorce, this is up to your discretion. I've been blessed to have managers who evolved into close friends and family. Maybe it's because I'm transparent and share aspects of my life on a high level. I usually choose to share because it gives the manager an understanding of why I might be less engaged with my team.

When you feel you're ready to handle questions and comments from family and friends, that may mean it's time to inform them of the pending divorce; it may not; it's always your call.

**Do not have the conversation until
you are equipped to manage the reaction.**

I don't know that I handled things gracefully regarding my in-laws. I shut down entirely, and they did too. I didn't attend family gatherings and didn't interact, but I wasn't invited either. If you had a relationship with in-laws and there are children involved, it's healthy to transition into an amicable relationship post-divorce, but it could take time. It's better for the children and a lot more beneficial for you and your ex-husband, as well. Be forewarned; they may hold some resentment towards you. Remember, divorce is drawing a proverbial line in the sand, and both sides are doling out blame.

Things can become adversarial. If that's in play, it will affect your ability to connect properly. Understand, they're hurting as well, and the divorce is likely triggering them to fight in response to the loss. Try not to get in the mud. Breathe and remain centered; this, too, shall pass.

During my divorce, I felt that a woman going through a divorce and trying to figure out her life didn't have a lot of time for convincing anyone of their innocence and goodwill. My position was that extended family and in-laws were welcomed to huddle around the children to maintain a relationship with them. Still, I chose the path of distancing myself, to keep as much of the peace as possible.

Remember, people follow your lead. If you've been complaining about your ex-husband for ten years and now want an amicable divorce, you're going to have to teach them how to have a new conversation with you about him. If you've been slinging mud for years, your girlfriends may need time to recondition and wrap their head around amicable, so show some grace there, too, when you can.

Concerning working with my ex-husband after the divorce, someone advised me to do something new concerning him. One year during tax refund season, my ex-husband asked if I'd give him a part of the return. My friend thought it was outrageous that he would even ask, considering how much more of the financial responsibility I had taken on. Still, I decided to use it as an opportunity to wave the white flag. I gave him $1,000 of the refund. My ex-husband was so appreciative; I could almost see his heart soften. He was taken aback and even whimpered a "wow, thanks." I effectively bought his heart and peace of mind for my family, all for the low, low price of $1,000. I could not continue to run a tab on him or keep a tally of wrongs and insufficiencies. I had to clear all charges on him. Likewise, some friends learned that I wasn't making him pay child support because I didn't want that to be the reason he supported his children. Nor did I want my children's father caught up in a system that was not designed to help him. That decision caused me to have to take up the slack on a few things, but that motivated a new personal standard, and I received an immediate raise at work! No need will ever go unmet when you're in alignment with your Source.

> Challenge yourself not to rely on your ex-husband's
> growth to improve and elevate your life, but rely
> on your personal development, so you'll make
> choices that attract the things that serve
> your greatest and highest good.

Yes, we want him to grow and mature, but know he has his own set of choices, and we need to abdicate our roles as God and mother over our husbands and ex-husbands. Whether they do the right thing or not, we have the power to create miracles for ourselves – even when our girlfriends think we've lost our minds.

Forgiving Your Ex

Our goal is to heal to the point that we no longer feel contentious. When we are courageous enough to take the bullseye off our ex's forehead and take a closer look at ourselves, refusing to be the victim, we prepare the way for healing and beneficial outcomes.

One has to be a victim to have contention with someone because someone has to be right, and someone has to be wrong. However, this Divine feminine process requires a level of spiritual maturity that's not for the weak at heart because it calls you up to manage intense, negative impulses from a place of sovereignty. From this place, you choose to love, even when there's no ostensible reason to choose love. This path sounds unrealistic because we're sometimes furious and highly emotional, so to choose a peaceful response for your family's well-being proves that you are in your sovereignty. It's groundbreaking when you cease pursuing vindication and believe that your focus is better served on what you're creating rather than tit for tat. The grace and mercy you sow now will later reap in your own life.

Sometimes it's only a matter of keeping up our boxing gloves just because fighting is what we do and how we relate to one another. No offense to our wonderful brothers out there, but women are arguably uniquely equipped and conditioned by society to be the bigger person. Whether it's fair or a bit of a burden, the Divine Feminine's energy and essence are saturated with grace, mercy, and healing. Sometimes we will need to leverage this skill to find a way to be more amicable, even when it hasn't been earned. As I healed, I no longer felt the sting of my ex-husbands blows. They were less unnerving. I saw his attacks as him projecting. He had unhealed trauma that caused him to say or do whatever, and I just so happened to be on the receiving end of it. Sometimes I would lash out and fight back, but those times became fewer because I learned my lashing out was my trauma rearing its head, and instead of letting it rule the moment, I shut my mouth, went within, and grabbed lessons from Vishen Lakhiani, Florence Scovel Schinn or Shanel Cooper-Sykes.

The Pain of Gossip

If you fear how someone will perceive you, consider that it's a misaligned focus. The good news is that anxiety is easily shifted when you clarify the reasons for your concern.

Who are you trying to be? Who are you trying to appease? Who do you need to satisfy?

Everything is a mirror. Everything we choose, every relationship, and action is a mirror to our mindset and priorities. When our mirror is the Creator, we tend to make Divine choices, but when we choose the god of public opinion, we corrupt every choice, every great idea, inspiration, and activity that downgrades our journey.

Satisfy your purpose by *only* comparing your
life to the mirror and opinion of the Higher Power!

What would God say about this thing or that thing? What does the Higher Power mean for me to learn about the divorce? Ask questions that trigger answers that point to consciousness and clarity.

One thing to consider is that other people's opinions are a lot more tormenting when you fail to have well-thought-out judgments of your own. Or worse yet, you have self-defeating beliefs that are soaked in the acid of regret. Ask yourself, what is the benefit of regret. You made the choices you made with the information you had at the time. Be sure not to linger too long in the space of second-guessing your choices. Linger, instead, in the space of better understanding, healing trauma, forgiveness, and letting things go. There's absolutely no way to correct past choices, so what you can do is look at things in the future. Determine how to make the situation the best that it can be today.

Honestly, things seem like a huge deal, but if you keep in mind that everyone walking the planet has their mess. Each of us broke the rules and made choices crossways of what others suggested. Ultimately, this is what *your* journey looks like and your choices, even the less than favorable ones, are how you learn.

People's opinion is their journey –
let them have it.

Years ago, if you could have crystal-balled it and got the outcome at the start, how would it have affected things? If God told you, early on, that you would get married at twenty-four years old and that it would last for twelve years, would you have taken it on? If God told you, the marriage would fall apart miserably. Still, you'd have memorable experiences, learn valuable insight that will propel you into your destiny, and birth wonderful children. Would you have been up for the task? What if the Creator further explained that people would frown upon you, and some may even gloat?

Well, would you sign up if God promised to repurpose every experience for your highest good?

That you would be covered because God is your source, and, in the end, you would grow to be more like the Creator – walking in higher power and strength. Would everything be worth it, then? Who knows?

The unknown is a humbling thing, but you'll get your bearings if you step into your creative power. Stop to determine how you want to see this thing shake out.

Forget everything that happened before this point and realize that you will likely live another 4 to 5 decades, depending on your current age. What do you want that to look like – what's the climax to the story?

This is the part of the movie when everyone grabs their seat and wonders how the protagonist will turn everything around. There's the downward spiral, the breakdown, the betrayal of a friend, the loss, and then the triumph. Dust yourself off, correct any misaligned focus, and ride into the sunset by doing the spiritual work to create desired outcomes.

Some people may gloat and jeer regarding your divorce, but those people have such disdain and heartache in their own lives that their demented reaction is proof they are deflecting and projecting.

They are the ones that need a helping hand, prayer, grace, mercy, and forgiveness. You're in a better place than they already.

Healthy people know we are all one. If I'm healthy, it augments your health. Your happy marriage affects our community, and in contrast, when things go wrong in your life, it affects the world. So, healthy people believe it's never good when someone suffers.

The level of misery and brokenness inside a person is evident by their reaction to other people's bad news and pain. While there is a human moment offense, wherein you'll think of a few choice words regarding their mean-spirited behavior, be even quicker to release the negative opinion altogether.

It's as if the gossiper and naysayer are physically sick and on life support. If they were terminal and stuck in a hospital bed and they were incessantly malicious and spiteful, you wouldn't exert any energy defending yourself or fighting back because you'd know they were dying and miserable. You would feel pity, and it would be a simple thing to deflect what they said and their opinion.

Granted, you likely won't wake up in the morning and begin to bless those that spitefully use and verbally abuse you. It's a process but understand it's necessary for your ascension as you own your Divine feminine power. Shed the need for validation, knowing that your worth comes from inside and above and never from other human beings.

What Our Friends Think

My Grandmother passed some information down that my mother repeated to me. She said that your friends change when you get married because you don't have single friends when you get married. You begin to do things with other married folks and couples. As it happened, I only developed a few friendships with other women during my marriage. I had my sorority sisters, but that was it.

Once I got married, I wasn't very active with the sorority and clung to my husband and his family. His sisters became my family. I would talk to them, confide, and share things with them, and they were my support and connection. We didn't go out with other couples very much either. We didn't have friends in common. So much of my social interaction was with blood relatives.

That's because I grew up interacting with cousins rather than friends from school. The family was sufficient for me, and that tendency found its way into my married life. Family members were my friends. So, during the divorce, the loss was significant.

Post-divorce, I had to learn to stand on my own and even distance myself, which was a great lesson in self-reliance. It's a matter of timing.

> If your pain from divorce is still raw,
> distancing yourself to be free from answering
> sensitive questions or looking to others for
> validation could prove to be a form of self-care.

We all want to be consoled during a divorce. The 5-year-old inside us wants to know that everyone supports our side of the argument, but sometimes friends, especially mutual friends, will choose a side on their own. I decided to disengage for a measure to save myself the heartache of rejection or scrutiny.

If your community is healthy and have wise friends, elders, and family that gather around you to support you positively, you're blessed. Lean into that village. Otherwise, distancing yourself may be best while you're in such a vulnerable state.

I didn't have to manage my friends during this time. I only had a few, and they were 100% supportive of whatever I needed at the time.

Point being, always be real with yourself and assess what your needs are. You're in a volatile position, so make sure you keep yourself in an environment that resonates with the label "handle with care."

At a certain point during the divorce, I did not feel there would be a winning point. I didn't feel I'd make it out of it in one piece. It seemed like the end of the world, and there would be no way to survive it. I asked God how to make it. I prayed that God would send me wise counsel who would help guide me in a way that I could quickly receive. I prayed for a shoulder on which to cry. I asked for the person who would lift my head and square my shoulders to face life again.

Soon enough, co-workers and girlfriends showed up in my life. Women with similar experiences, even one girlfriend who lost her children's father at an early age as I did, began to spring up to hold me up in the struggle. I have a friend who is twenty years my senior, a counselor by trade, and who proved to be a gift direct from God. She was my angel and carried me in her wings to the other side of the divorce, single mom' ing, and the death of my ex-husband.

These particular friends were good at giving me space to be enraged, to be sad and hopeless, and to sulk. They always gently redirected my focus and helped elevate my energy about things. Manifest friends who think righteously, to hold space for you. Looking around your friend group and don't see anyone of this stature? It's ok; set your intention, be open to receive, and watch how you attract your angels to you.

Releasing Resentment

I never spent any length of time without a man. Since the eleventh grade, I've always had a boyfriend or boyfriends. After marriage, I desperately wanted someone in that spot. I was addicted to attention and didn't know it. A good morning text or a random checking on me call throughout the day were familiar gestures to which I'd become accustomed. So rather than allow me time to attract a bond from a healthy place, codependent Viv ran the show. You may want to be alone for a while, a long while, or indefinitely. However, when you begin to think about new horizons for your love life, don't circumvent the healing process.

Do the work and give yourself the gift of presenting your Divine feminine Goddess energy to the world—a woman who is whole and complete. A woman who has gone through the fire, and like the phoenix, she rises from the ashes.

Believing that a loving man exists for you is the first part of meeting him.

A positive mindset is a strong compass that points true north toward your best outcomes. Faith and positivity will find your wealth; better health, and it's how you find love.

Energetically, we meet everyone in the spirit before we physically see them with our eyes.

Meeting someone in the flesh is the revelation or expression of where we are spiritually and energetically. So, when you meet Mr. Amazing, it's after you've fallen in love with yourself and realized your Ms. Amazing. Again, by the time you are in the same country, city, and room with someone, both of you have believed long enough that the other existed to manifest the opportunity. This dynamic is in play for the dream guy, as well as the nightmare.

Be advised – you are creating experiences right now as you read this sentence in this book. Charge your thoughts with desirable outcomes. Speak to the heart of the man before you even meet him. Pray over his life, finances, health, and happiness.

Love him
before you meet him.

To do that more fully means giving up the right to complain about the past and refusing to sign-on to disparaging remarks about men. Work relentlessly to stay observant and less reactive in the face of everyday negativity. Red lipstick and voluptuous cleavage catch a man's eye but inner radiance emanating from the essence of a woman who's whole captures his heart.

Clearing unhealthy thoughts about men and
focusing on what we desire increases
our love frequency. Our loving, tender
energy is a magnet and attracts men effortlessly.

This effervescent mindset only works free of resentment. I did the work, and I put it in this book for you. Do the work – complete the exercises in this book, attend seminars, and hire therapists and mentors to hold you accountable to a higher standard of mental health and emotional intelligence. Otherwise, you run the risk of meeting the right guy, only to tell him to take a hike in a fit of aggravation. Let your Divine feminine soften you and heal your heart. It will help you manage and transmute irritation, resentment, and fear, clearing the slate in your heart and mind in preparation for your new love.

List everyone you're holding resentment towards. When you've completed the list, call out each name individually and declare forgiveness and blessing over them - release them to their best life.

Process five names a day until the list is completed.

EXERCISE 6.1

Family	
1.	6.
2.	7.
3.	8.
4.	9.
5.	10.
Friends & Neighbors	
1.	6.
2.	7.
3.	8.
4.	9.
5.	10.
Supervisors/Managers	
1.	6.
2.	7.
3.	8.
4.	9.
5.	10.

Co-workers Colleagues	
1.	6.
2.	7.
3.	8.
4.	9.
5.	10.
Religious Leaders; Politicians; Deities; Teachers; Professionals	
1.	6.
2.	7.
3.	8.
4.	9.
5.	10.
Miscellaneous	
1.	6.
2.	7.
3.	8.
4.	9.
5.	10.

Mindset Mastery Exercise

Seven

The New You

*"If you don't fix the trauma, you are working
on the wrong thing."*
— Oprah (CBS This Morning)

You are at a place in your life where you decide what happens next. For some women, this will be the first time in their lives that they are "woke" enough to choose the life they live consciously. What type of woman do you want to present to the world? What experience are you attracting? The answers are on the other side of your mindset work and personal development. This chapter introduces some modalities that have proven to be a big fix in countless men and women's lives. Some essential tips designed to help you upgrade your standard of living and detailed instructions on certain significant modalities.

Be sure to consider what stage of the divorce journey you're in and select the modalities that suit your current status. Many things give life meaning, but any number of those things would be a curse if it's not the season of your life for it.

For example, many women will wisely ignore the option to date at this time. They know they need to forgive, clear negative energy, and heal. There will be a time to open up to new prospects, perhaps even marriage again, but many women will want to back-burner that option.

Nevertheless, if a man approaches during this time, please be gentle with your response.

The men may connect on a level that is helpful in some other way, a job connection, or maybe the man's father has a tire shop, and you happen to need a new set. Don't walk the planet as a "Bitter Betty." Having several different tools to help you heal and grow is necessary and one of those tools may include a healthy, platonic relationship with a nice guy. While your girlfriends are fun and supportive, no one and nothing replaces the energy of an upstanding, caring man. And that's beyond sexuality. Don't close yourself off from other people just because they have a phallus.

Kindness won't kill us as long as we know our boundaries and limitations. One of my favorite gurus talks about the high standard she has for men and how most men will never qualify for serious romantic consideration. But she always speaks to men from all walks of life and chats with guys in sincerity and tenderness. She doesn't blow them off disrespectfully or disregard their feelings. Men are humans, real-life people, and we're held accountable for how we treat them and everyone else. This topic leads us to a vital big fix tool: *karma*. Elevate what you do, say, and think – first regarding yourself, your family, your ex, and every sentient being.

You need good karma to live your best life!

Lifestyle

Lifestyle is not a matter of magic or good luck; it's intention, strategy, execution, and commitment. Everything begins with an intention. Be it consciously or unconsciously; we're making daily decisions according to what we hold as our intention. I perceive intentions as seeds, and it's these seeds of intentions that determine our life's harvest or experiences. For instance, when I held my ex-husband accountable for everything I deemed offensive, my garden was abundant with turmoil and anger. There was no peace, and my family stayed in fight or flight mode. We all walked around on the lookout for landmines and hand grenades.

Since my intention was accountability and persecution, my strategy was to tell my ex-husband everything he did wrong and how he should change to be better. My commitment for execution didn't waiver, and it seemed the more I critiqued, the more offensive his actions became. Alternatively, when my intention shifted to being a woman who exudes radiance, beauty, nurturing energy, and a magnetizing aura, I saw a completely different harvest. My strategy was to embody my God-like essence. I no longer needed anything because I was everything. I learned I had all the resources and answers within. Yes, I needed more money for my bills. Yes, I needed help with my kids, and yes, I needed to feel the love and passion from a man, but now my need stemmed from a desire, not a place of lack. I remember Shanel Cooper-Sykes explained this way of perceiving as if you're asking someone to hand you your purse. You'd simply say, please pass me my purse and expect that they'd give it to you. You wouldn't panic or worry if they'd hand it to you or not because you're lacking; you're desiring. The same energy holds true for anything you could want. It's already yours energetically; you're now merely requesting so you can move it into your physical being. I executed this strategy consistently and watched my garden begin to sprout and overtime, flourish.

Many people suffer from procrastination and self-sabotage, and they haven't realized that their excessive struggle to birth their dream is as simple as hiring a mentor, coach, or therapist. As women, we're conditioned to spend money on hair, nails, shoes, clothes, and handbags rather than purchasing a mentor's expertise. We're also trained to believe we don't need help, or we're inadequate if we need to pay someone to tell us what we "should" already know. However, successful men, athletes, entrepreneurs, millionaires, and billionaires perpetually publicly profess their use of consultants and coaches to keep on track, on schedule, and working optimally. Sometimes the best way to overcome your blocks is to leverage the help of a qualified expert. Remember our Einstein quote, "We cannot solve our problems with the same thinking we used when we created them."

Find a mentor specializing in the specific problem area – someone who will help you overcome the obstacles you face today. Whether it's finding love after divorce, rebranding, starting your business, or releasing weight, research, and interview candidates until you find the best fit. Finding the right mentor for where you are in life is a matter of aligning, asking, and allowing. When the student is ready, the teacher appears. Whenever it's time for me to pivot, I recognize I need wise counsel, and it's at that time I'll catch a podcast, or someone on YouTube will speak to my situation and prompt a chain of events. I'll call a friend, and during our conversation, they'll mention a resource for me to check out, and the result is I'll find the exact person who can help me move from where I am to where I want to be.

Understand that a mentor or a coach is not a friend or a cheerleader. A good mentor has several stealthy techniques to determine whether your lack of progress is due to a lack of wisdom, resources, or healing. They are laser-sharp in getting you to execute and achieve your goals.

Leverage mentors to fast-track your progress and realize your desired outcomes.

A thriving lifestyle could also include having colleagues that are high achievers, folks that offer professional tips, and have achieved what you desire to accomplish. It's helpful to hang out with people whose accomplishments make you feel a little nervous. Always being the smartest, most powerful person in the room could stunt your growth and prove to be an act of cowardice. Get out, and network in places were movers and shakers frequent. Practice introducing yourself – train yourself to feel at home in powerful spaces. Make acquaintance with great people. New, exciting people bring new, exciting energy into your life.

Connect with colleagues to expand your resources and exchange information. Remember, iron sharpens iron.

It's vital to maintain a clean and healthy home, car, office, etc. Surround yourself with things that you love – pieces that reflect your personal style and values. While you're reclaiming your rightful place as a Divine Goddess, purchase signs, paintings, and novelties with empowering idioms written on them – things that remind you to maintain elevated thoughts.

Provide the proper conditions which nurture you and allow your inner splendor to come forth.

Travel to new towns and countries. Go to places where the people dress differently, speak differently, eat, and have fun differently. Expand your horizons. Traveling can serve to reset your mind. After the divorce, you may find that feeding your psyche a sequence of new sites and pleasures provides a substantial emotional uplift. Travel triggers and rewires the brain and entices you to consider new possibilities and rediscover a sense of wonderment. Remember to check out Dr. Joe Dispenza on YouTube and read Breaking the Habit of Being Yourself to learn more about rewiring your brain.

**Feed your senses new experiences to expand
your thoughts and beliefs around what's possible for the next
phase of your journey.**

Divorce comes with obvious repercussions, and weight loss or gain is a common effect. Physical health is far more severe than fitting into your favorite dress. Nutrition is the Source of energy and vitality, and being disease-free is a quintessential component of a quality lifestyle. Your mindset and subsequent behavior are affected by what you eat. Have you ever heard someone blame low blood sugar for a nasty attitude? Remember the hilarious Snickers commercials? The 'hangry' (hungry + angry) vibe is real. Take care of yourself nutritionally; this supports your efforts to avoid unnecessary blow-ups with your ex-husband, shouting at the kids, and confrontations at work. Consider curbing any addiction to caffeine, alcohol, sugar, and fast foods. I see my Internal Medicine Doctor (IMD) annually to ensure my levels are normal and get advice on what to look out for.

In 2018 I felt depressed and had zero energy. I couldn't figure out what was wrong. I went to therapy, saw a neurologist, increased my meditation practice, and none of it helped me out of the funk. I saw my IMD, and after running labs, I discovered my iron level was a 7. The lowest it should be is 15, so I was severely lacking, and my system was in distress. The doctor recommended I take an iron supplement and told me my lack of iron (anemia) caused me to have low energy. He described it as a car with no fuel - no matter how many bells, whistles, and features the vehicle has, without fuel, it doesn't start, and it's impossible to move. I believe I benefitted from talk therapy, Neurotherapy, and meditating, but the core issue for my funky state was I needed iron. I ate plenty of fruits, veggies, and high-quality protein, drank 7-10 cups of water daily, and exercised, but still lacked motivation. It took professional help to fix my issues.

Visit your doctor regularly, discuss your lifestyle, and get their feedback and recommendations as you take steps to enhance your health and manage your stress.

See your doctor regularly to know how your inners are functioning and what you can do to restore yourself to your optimal state.

Be mindful of the films and TV shows you watch, and remember they may be a part of the matrix that misinforms your outlook on life. Consider having a low-tolerance for hostile media for your post-divorce lifestyle. You'd be surprised how aggressive lyrics in music creep into your psyche, wreaking havoc on your optimism and attitude. Cultivate a taste for uplifting films with inspiring endings. Rom-coms, sci-fi, action, and adventure movies helped me feel good when I took time out for entertainment. I also love documentaries produced by positive thought leaders and *Super Soul Sunday.* I let go of the low-energy alternatives because they didn't add value to my life.

Be intentional with everything your five senses take in, including media. Everything is energy, and energy is always transferring. Be selective and choose what best serves what you're calling into your life.

Feeding your spirit is as important as feeding your body. Find ways to tap into your inner being and plug into the Source of your existence. My spiritual practice includes a morning ritual of meditating, journaling, praying, and ranting. I do this to ground and center, to start my day on full and with intention. My evening ritual consists of the morning ritual plus reading, sacred showers, dancing, and stretching in front of a mirror. Church or spiritual fellowships provide inspiring messages and community which provide support during a divorce.

Maintain a spiritual routine to support your mind, body, soul, and womb as you create your new life as a woman who is whole, perfect, and complete.

Celebrate your feminine divinity in the spiritual sense by establishing self-care rituals. I believe every woman would benefit from having a copy of Sacred Pampering Principles by Debrena Jackson Gandy on her nightstand, bookshelf, or bathroom. Debrena explains the importance of setting aside time for your inner renewal. Regular detox baths, slowly oiling your body, sacred prayer, and meditation time are a few of her recommended refueling techniques. In her book, she explains the items you'll need and gives the step by step instructions.

As you invest in your inner health, you may also find it beneficial to pamper yourself regularly. Get your hair and nails done, go for brunch or tea with your girlfriends, get regular massages and pedicures. Wear clothes that make you feel sexy and vibrant – play with color, fabrics, and design. Wear beautiful nightgowns to bed and remind yourself that you are worth dressing up whether someone's in your bed or not. Dress up for yourself and don't neglect your self-care and beauty regimen.

You deserve a sacred self-care ritual; your future self and your legacy need you to be whole, celebrated, and sovereign.

Just Breathe

• •

Meditation and breathwork saved me from a life of trauma and fight or flight. In the spring of 2019, I began a series of Neurotherapy treatments for anxiety and PTSD. What I learned through a process called brain mapping was meditation is the fix. Brain mapping monitors brain waves, and the therapist tells you whether you're in alpha, beta, theta, etc. These are terms that describe if you're calm and creative or in fight or flight. As Dr. Joe explains in his books, it isn't time to dream and create when you're in fight or flight mode. Your survival is depending on your next action. The problem is we often live in fight or flight mode even when we're not in danger; fight or flight has become our default state. Since I had been meditating for several years, I knew how to get into theta, but I didn't have proof that I was in theta until I received the brain mapping scans from my neurologist. The scans showed my brain activity for a period of 30 minutes. As you might guess, the first five minutes, my waves were alpha and beta, but as time went on, my waves slowed down, and I moved from high beta to theta. I felt calm, centered, unhurried, unbothered, and capable of managing my life.

I tell anyone who will listen, intentionally breathe, and meditate. I start every meeting by asking the participants to take a couple of deep cleansing breaths. This simple action directly impacts the brain and the body in a positive way.

Rebounding from divorce while becoming a single mother and having to rediscover both your personal and professional purpose as an individual can be overwhelming and even debilitating. I offer you the gift of meditation and breathwork to assist you through your journey with hopes that you emerge from the ashes better and more robust.

Self-care is work, and I ask you to invest in your
self-care in a way you may have never invested before.
What you formerly did may have gotten you this far,
but who you're becoming as a result of this disruption may
require you to go deeper into yourself, for yourself.

The life you want may not be accessible with old tools. Consider renewing your mind and learning new information for this next phase of your journey. You can stay where you are emotionally, financially, health-wise, etc., but I suspect you're reading this book out of a hunger to transcend your current state. If so, then let's master the gift of calmness, the power of intention, and the art of allowing.

The heart, mind, and body work in concert, and the breath is the connector between the three parts. When the heart and mind agree in peace and love, it's sometimes referred to as coherence; and *the meditative breath facilitates that state*. When the heart, mind, and body achieve calmness, the peace it yields is rejuvenating.

Meditation silences the chatter from the mind and helps to tranquilize the impulses from the body. It softens the heart's emotions and quiets the voice of anxiety—Use meditation regularly to center yourself and to break the habits that no longer serve who you are and what you're creating.

For beginners, start with a basic 5-minute meditation to learn how to sit still in silence. As you sit, you'll notice distracting thoughts. Simply bring your attention to your breath, and let the thoughts come and go. As you bring your attention to your breath, you allow your body to relax. Over time you'll feel a sense of peace and calm.

Commit to scheduling a set-time to test-out the meditation exercise at the end of this chapter. Remember to schedule ongoing meditation exercises on your calendar. Pulling this new habit into your daily lifestyle is the challenging part, more so than the actual practice of meditating. Be vigilant, believing that it's worth the inconvenience and like Nike says, just do it!

Check out Oprah and Deepak Chopra's meditation app and their series of 21-day meditations. It was their 21-day series that introduced me to meditation and subsequently changed my life.

Fasting

As mentioned, I manifested my dream job during a forty-day fast. During the fast, I made peace with where I was, fully committed to mindset and forgiveness exercises, corrected self-talk and thoughts, and carried out new behaviors.

I began this particular fast on Good-Friday, and before Lent ended, I received the job offer. I started working a week later, so the timeline for this manifestation was within 40 days.

For me, fasting works because it makes me focus on what I'm trying to achieve. For example, if I'm fasting and have an intense craving for the food or thing I'm abstaining from, I affirm the goal. I use the urge as an alarm or reminder to focus on my intention. I use the energy of the desire to fuel my commitment to being, doing, and having whatever I intended as the focus of the fast.

I let the appetite and craving be a cue to affirm the reasons for the fast.

The craving is an invitation to come back to center and recommit to your goal. Fasting works because the body's natural desires and impulses are repurposed as an alarm and indicator, prompting you to center and put your attention on what you're manifesting. A reminder to renew your mindset and review the affirmations that help bring you out of reactive mode and into your intention.

Specifically, during a craving, I would rant or write a statement of appreciation (i.e., acknowledging I'm operating from I have and I am and not I want or don't have). I would also meditate and create a mind movie seeing my desires play out on the screen of my mind.

During the Lent fast, I gave up sugar, wine, caffeine, TV, and social media. I began that fast while still working at a job that wasn't my favorite place in the world. I drank peppermint tea instead of coffee in the mornings. Physically, I craved the coffee's stimulation to help me get in gear to show up for this job, but spiritually I was called to not self-medicate and use my internal resources to fuel my day.

I would let the smell of the peppermint in the tea remind me to be appreciative. I made the scent a trigger for me to go into gratitude and praise. In between my hot peppermint tea sips, I would speak the list of things for which I was praying and speak gratitude for that which I had – I behaved as if I already had the physical form of what I desired.

I would pray and meditate in the mornings and the evenings. I would also meditate whenever I got an urge to break the fast.

I believe fasting worked for me because I declared peace with where I was in my life. I made peace with my ex-husband and even made peace with the job, despite my interest in moving. I did not entertain thoughts of pity, but I shifted those thoughts to what I was creating. I also didn't obsess. For instance, if I went to a restaurant, I would adhere to the fast, but I did not count it as a failure if the marinara sauce had sugar. It was not fast for the sake of health or religious observance.

I abstained from certain things to trigger the cravings that would remind me to realign and go back into the space of balance. Even if you slip and break the fast, don't berate yourself; be gentle with you. As for the haters in your life, ignore them. Fasting is an internal, reflective sacred practice. Hold yourself accountable, find support and mentorship to help keep you accountable, but be gentle with yourself and keep it sweet. If you fail and fall off, get up, brush yourself off, and get back to fasting.

How Long Before I See Results?

In my experience, manifesting is about belief and action. I could manifest a sandwich or a house. It all depends on my level of belief, actions, and ability to detach from the results. I learned there were things that, arguably, were indeed possible, but because it was too big of a leap for my belief system, I was merely causing myself frustration. I learned if my desires were something comparable to my faith-level, I would see physical signs of manifestation sooner than if I held disbelief in my energy.

EXERCISE 7.1

Meditation Practice

1. Sit in a comfortable space, free of distraction.

2. Close your eyes or have a soft gaze.

3. Set a timer with a tranquil alarm tone.

    a. Beginners start with a 5-minute meditation.

    b. Consistency is what matters at this point – not length of time.

    c. Meditate every day for 5-minutes.

    d. Increase the time as you feel led with a goal of 15 minutes.

4. Try breathing in through your nose and exhaling through your mouth.

5. Hold a soft smile to encourage the release of endorphins.

6. Optional: select a mantra or meditative word and hold the feeling and energy of that single word as you meditate.

    a. This helps focus your thoughts.

    b. Sample words: serenity, peace, ease, harmony, tranquility, bliss, grace, calm.

7. Breathe in slowly and notice the pull of air into your nose and the expanse of your belly.

    a. Your belly will expand out on the inhale, and deflate inward on the exhale.

    b. Optional: breathe in for 6 counts and exhale for 12 counts to exhale completely.

c. Optional:

    i.   inhale for specific count,

    ii. gently hold the breath for 3 counts,

    iii. exhale for nearly double the inhale count.

Tip: Seemingly positive words like "god" or "love" have both negative and positive triggers for some people, so use words that induce harmony.

EXERCISE 7.2

Meditation Practice – Kids & Family

Practice meditation as a family, either daily or weekly – but maintain a consistent schedule. Invite everyone, including the children, to sit silently in a room together in peace and serenity. Your first session may be a simple 3 to 5-minute silent meditation depending on the children's ages.

You may want to employ incentives whereby everyone that sits silently in meditation for a specific amount of time gets a treat.

Periodically extend the length of time of the meditations.

If you have an infant or toddler, you may elect to make a deal with the other household members that you will all practice meditation together when the baby takes a nap, or you will take turns caring for the baby while the others practice.

You may be amazed at how well children adapt and embrace a meditation regimen and how it influences their overall behavior and mindset.

EXERCISE 7.3

Fasting Exerciser

Action 1: Write your Fast Declaration and post on a wall or your bathroom mirror, then take a picture of it with your cell phone or other digital device to reference. Or type it using Google docs and take a screenshot.

- What is the purpose of my fast?
- From what am I abstaining?
- What is the duration of the fast?

Action 2:
- Pray and meditate in the morning.
- Pray and meditate in the evening.
- During Cravings
  - o Review your fast declaration with an attitude of appreciation.
  - o During your fast, tap into the feeling of how you'll feel when you have what you're desiring manifest.
  - o Ask/Pray for revelations, keep an open mind and write down what you hear/receive.

Bonus Chapter
A Child's Perspective

"Each day of our lives we make deposits in the memory banks of our children."
— Charles R. Swindoll
Evangelical Christian Pastor

My children are a great light in my life. I adore them and realize that I am a steward and guide for their lives. The divorce affected each child differently. There were some basic commonalities, but each child had their takeaways regarding the experience. As a Mom, I watched over each child's growth, hovering as much as possible to help ensure they could get through the unfamiliar territory and new family dynamic.

My daughter Lauren was ten years old during the divorce. She was devasted and could not understand why we had to live separately. I witnessed her decline in grades, lashing out in school, and knew we had to find a way to get ahead of things. I grappled with setting a balance between grace and discipline, considering all she was handling emotionally.

We decided to enroll her in empowerment activities like *Young Women's Inc.* The Program helped her step into leadership by engaging her love of writing as a vehicle to express anger, sadness, and confusion. It provided an opportunity to be heard, and I believe that as she saw her work inspire others, it gave her an added incentive to walk in excellence and leadership. Today, she has a full-time job and is in college full time working toward her goals and exploring options. She has a bright light and a level of self-mastery level that was cultivated through her rising above the disappointment of her parent's divorce.

My son Robert's reaction to the divorce was anger, confusion, and feelings of betrayal. He was nine years old at the time of the divorce, and he wouldn't accept that his father and I could not work things out and would not be able to live together. He hated living between two separate houses. As parents, I knew we would need to be mature enough to help him find peace with the process, especially since none of the children asked for this experience. Thankfully, we soon discovered that my son's love of sports would help pull him through. He became self-reliant and honed a transferrable skill of using adversity as fuel for his goals. He learned how to redirect anger and pain – to transmute emotion, and I know that ability will be a ready tool for the rest of his life. He graduated high school in 2019, works full-time, and is in college. He exercises religiously and blows me away with his demonstrations of physical and mental strength.

Ryan, my youngest son, was a tender three years old during the divorce, and I wasn't at all surprised by his sadness. He adored his father, and how could he possibly understand why we lived separately. His confusion broke my heart. For him, I nurtured him as much and as often as possible. He was born with such a bright light, and I felt guilty and prayed my decision didn't cause his light to go out. I took some solace in knowing he was resilient and logical beyond his years. Even as a child, Ryan was "woke," and I knew that gift would serve his ability to find his footing. Today he's in middle school and eats, sleeps, and breathes video games. He idolizes his big brother, even when he makes him do push-ups, and loves being spoiled by his big sister.

The following is commentary from my kids about the divorce. I hope hearing a child's perspective helps you as you guide your children through the rough waters of divorce and that it shines a light at the end of the tunnel for the family.

Lauren M. Gardner, 19 Years Old

If you're reading this book, you are probably wondering why a woman would want to be friends with their ex-husband. But I need you to breakdown that wall and be open to this! The importance that this topic has on the success of your family is crucial! When you hold onto your anger toward someone, it blocks your blessings. It's baggage.

I won't lie to you, though; it takes a lot of time and strength.

Trust me, I know because I watched my parents go from being the power couple and "relationship goals" couple to becoming two people who couldn't even talk about groceries or grades.

But thankfully, they went from arguing all the time to being friends and only arguing some time.

They began looking out for each other and believe it or not; it became a must for my dad to meet anyone my mom dated. The craziest thing was when my mom met who my dad was dating, and they became friends.

Some may turn their faces up to that one and may even say that it's crazy but take it from me; it really happened, and it can happen for you too.

The shift made the energy between us so different. It wasn't as stressful as it had been.

Now, I am the oldest of three, the only girl, and as such, the most qualified to be the boss of everything amongst my siblings. I can truly say my brothers and I had a better life after my mom and dad started getting along.

As long as I can remember, my Mom and Dad always referred to the saying in the movie Ice Age, "That's what you do in a herd."

They taught me that no matter what the family goes through, be it arguments, fights, or anything that life throws at us, family is family.

For the health of the "herd," divorced parents have to find a way to create a relationship built on love and forgiveness. I hope and wish every child of divorced parents have the chance to experience that type of love from the people who mean the most - the parents.

Robert C. Gardner III, 18 Years Old

Imagine the life of the Will Smith character from the Fresh Prince of Bel-Air TV series. He moved from a negative location to a lavish and premium home. We might think he had a come up, moving into a big house and living rich. There's nothing like clearing the slate and leaving the past behind. It seemed as if he lived a life that any kid would love. But as the series progressed, we learned that there was so much more to Will's story.

In one episode, Will meets his father for the first time, and before anyone jumps to conclusions – wondering where I'm going with this, I knew my father very well, thank you. During this scene, a very real pain could be seen. There was an agony that was held within the character.

I related to that episode because, as a kid, our family bounced from home to home.

However, being a glass-half-full personality, I chose to see moving as an adventure. I started out excited by the possibilities. Outwardly, I was a kid with an exciting life of luxury and new beginnings. But like Will, I harbored a hidden pain that I did not initially comprehend. There was a tug on my heart each time I had to leave old friends to go make new ones.

Moving caused a longing for lost relationships that I was not fully prepared to master. I looked like a happy Fresh Prince of Bel-Air character, but deep down, I was wounded. Eventually, I developed a resistance to moving altogether, and my social skills began to subside. I even failed to relate to members of my family. Because of my dilemma, it took a long time to realize I wasn't the only person in pain.

My mother weathered many storms, from divorce to the sudden death of a loved one. I've witnessed the best and worst of it all. It's so easy to get caught up, letting bad moments create an aura of darkness - making us forget all the good that life gives us. That darkness may last for years, and it travels with us regardless of relocations and attempts to restart our lives.

What I learned is that tragedy brings the gift of wisdom.

Granted, I wish I would have gotten that gift from an easier lesson, something other than divorce or death. But I see that the pain is sometimes how we earn our victory. Death and loss can stir up love and unity, but first, there may be some heaven and hell to go through.

During the beginning of the divorce, I witnessed a house divided, occupied by people with empty hearts. There was a period of time that saw all of us as wanderers. We walked our paths blindfolded and misguided by anger, grief, and depression. What was being passed off as self-sufficiency turned out to be our pride and egos. We isolated ourselves from the world, and worse, from one another. It was our version of that climactic scene from the sitcom, the part of the series, when we could no longer pretend to be happy and joyful. It was the part of our story where we showed the pain we carried.

My Dad used to tell us, "That's what we do in a herd." His words would replay in my head always, as I wondered if my father was trying to teach me something from the grave. My Dad never missed a game, that is until he got sick. I could always look in the stands and know without a doubt; I'd see him sitting there, cheering for me. It was true that our family had a way of doing things. I understood that my mother was trying to be strong for us, but I could still see her struggle. My heart was breaking during the divorce and the death of my Dad too. So much so that I would choke-up every time I tried to tell my Mom how proud I was of her ability to keep going. She would attend our games at school, and I tried not to show the pain of no longer seeing my father in the stands alongside the family.

The toughest part was needing to talk to my Mom, but not knowing how. I would hold things in my heart to fester.

I remember the screaming arguments and hurt feelings between us. I recall the voice in my head that begged me to stop shouting at my mother, and then the stubborn need to win an argument and have my say.

There was a time when I wanted out – to move out on my own, having convinced myself that my mother's problems had become too big for her to see my pain. I also remember trying to make my mom proud, but I felt that my efforts fell flat every time. My social skills, empathy, and connection had abandoned me, and there was a time when I was a raw nerve.

Everything she said or did hurt me, and the only thing I wanted to do was hurt her in return. Crazy, isn't it? I had gone from that jovial, fun-loving Will Smith character to a wounded, wayward soul.

Things changed as I began to pray for my Mom every night. I asked that God would ease her heartache and help her. I prayed that she would somehow know how grateful I was to have her. I hoped that even though I had distanced myself, that our relationship wouldn't dwindle and fall away. I had plans to make a name for myself, to make a way to care for my mother, regardless of the rift between us. I was, and remain, my mother's #1 fan.

My prayer life began to bring comfort that can only be described as miraculous.

I began to feel guided by the Spirit as new ideas came to mind – things that helped me a lot.

For example, each night, I began to blow-out as many push-ups as I could before going to bed. It may sound goofy, but that simple act changed my life. It was a way to get tension from each day out of my body.

Through it all, I learned that being strong is knowing how to navigate weakness.

I learned that there's nothing like suppressing the heartache.

I also learned that sometimes you make room for loved ones, especially when they're hurting.

There are statistics chasing so many of us, from alcohol-related tragedy, gang banging, drug dealing, crazy partying, and irresponsible lifestyles. At a certain point, I had to decide to make the best choices, rejecting certain options to rebel. I had to rewrite my own episode and TV series with a happier, smarter ending.

And not because everything's fine but because I learned to be okay despite the pain.

I tell my brother, and other guys that closed mouths don't get fed. We have to speak into our lives, praying and asking for the miracles that will heal our situation. We have to do the work. My mother taught me to try not to be the pain in other women's lives and refuse to treat them any way other than how I would want someone treating my mom or sister. It's not easy, but if we don't make the better choice, if we don't heal, we don't pray and believe - if we don't do the necessary grinding, who will care for our families?

So, I am quick to tell other guys to remember that their mother is, *first*, a human. Although she may appear to be a superhero, she can't be perfect. And I teach them to appreciate things about life that are fun. But most of all, to also embrace the episodes that require us to show the pain and agony under the surface. I tell them how I learned to love and care for my family.

Ultimately, I learned that life is a marathon, and we all run it together – "that's what we do in the herd."

Ryan C. Gardner, 11 Years Old

I hope to help some parents and kids by saying what I really feel. I understand divorce is when two people use to love each other but separate because they either don't love each other anymore or because of some other reason.

Some kids may think the divorce is their fault, but I don't think that. It couldn't be my fault because I was too young to have anything to do with it. I was around three years old, so things clearly happened before I was even born. While I know my parents' divorce had nothing to do with me, I do encourage other children, no matter their age, to understand that parents make choices on their own.

> The children shouldn't assume that there is anything that they could do to change a parent.

I never really tried to figure out ways to get my Mom and Dad back together as I got older because I wanted them to be happy. So, if being together made them sad, then that's the last thing I would ever help happen. I just wanted our family to be as tight as possible, and I knew it wasn't necessary to have married parents.

> My parents divorced each other, but they didn't divorce the family.

I also believe some children may feel sad or embarrassed about their parent's divorce. But I think that's not smart because divorce is so common. I think a lot of parents deal with marriage problems, adultery, and sometimes divorce, but it's always the parent's choice. So, there is no reason to take divorce personally and be disappointed.

195

My advice to kids who have parents who are divorcing is to make sure they stay positive and good.

> **Because if the kids stay positive, their parents
> will be in a better place, whether they actually
> get the divorce or get back together.**

The most important thing is for the children to learn how to stay in a positive mood.

Children of divorce should hang out with friends and get the kind of best friends that help them remain positive. They should ask their mom and dad to allow them to hang out with the right people and make their own community of friends - play video games and have a life of their own.

EXERCISE 8.1

Writing Catharsis for Kids

Action: Take the children to the store and let them pick out a writing pad or journal, a special pen & highlighter. Add some stickers to the mix so they can pick the ones that emphasize some of the things they write.

Action: Get some treats & find a quiet place at home for a writing exercise.

Action: Take 30 minutes to sit with them, have them write, and discuss their comments.

Tip: DON'T JUDGE OR BULLY.

It's a time for the children's release, even if their feelings don't condone your actions or stroke your ego. Just hold the space for them to allow their thoughts and feelings to flow. Be prepared for a few contractions and some discomfort but support them as this is all about their journey.

Side Note: You may want to schedule a massage or meditation session for yourself sometime later in the day to de-stress.

Note: You may be surprised to learn some of the emotions that children harbor as witnesses to a dissolving marriage. Seek additional help on helping them clear negative energy so they won't repeat the choices, the errors, and the circumstances they witnessed.

Note: Before you work with your children, work on yourself concerning clearing bitterness, playing the blame game, having vendettas, and refusing to apologize for your mistakes. If you go into this like a warlord or angel, the kids will likely shut down. If you don't show some level of emotional risk and transparency, why should they risk anything?

Note: Depending on the dynamics between siblings, you may want to have separate sessions with each child or have them all meet together for this exercise. My children enjoyed both together and in private time.

Questions for Your Children to Allow Them to Express Themselves (Be certain the exercise is advisable by your child's psychologist or medical professional)

1. Write how you feel right now.

———————————————————————

2. Write 5 words that describe your mom.

———————————————————————

3. Write 5 words that describe your dad.

———————————————————————

4. Write 5 words that describe how you feel about your family.

———————————————————————

5. What's the most difficult thing about this time in your life?

———————————————————————

6. What's the most exciting thing about this time in your life?

———————————————————————

7. What do you want your mom and dad to know?

———————————————————————

Mindset Mastery Exercise

Epilogue

Appreciation

"Be thankful for what you have; you'll end up having more. If you concentrate on what you don't have, you will never, ever have enough."
—Oprah Winfrey

My ex-husband died on May 16, 2018, after battling cancer. It was unexpected and life changing. The weird thing about it is that we had just gotten our relationship to a really good place about 2 to 3 years before his passing. Things were ridiculously calm. We were doing really well. The fights were fewer, and we had taken the word amicable to a whole new level. We both worked hard to enjoy a positive co-parenting life. My ex would participate in my coaching camps and workshops, and he also promoted my events and brought in clients. Whenever a teacher would call me, I'd immediately ask them to hold while I conferenced in my ex because it was important to me that the teachers knew our children had a present father. We rarely made decisions about the kids solo and took pride in how well we partnered on kid-related things.

We were all at the hospital visiting when he began to have complications, and the children were by his side when he took his last breath. Our kids were devastated; we all were.

After he passed away, I had to process my emotions, the good and the bad. I sometimes felt that he got let off the hook. I even asked God why I couldn't die, and he be the one left behind to take care of the kids on his own. I felt inept and had no will to try to figure out how to help my children survive this immeasurable loss. I felt incredulous. I know it sounds dysfunctional, but many women who are made to be single mothers are maddened by the thought of the undertaking and can hardly believe they are being forced to take on parenting alone.

I believed my ex, and I would be grandparents together, so I couldn't grasp what life was supposed to look like when he passed away, and we still had school-aged children.

We don't love someone because they don't have any flaws; we find ways to love them in spite of their flaws. Now that's really what we do in the herd.

I felt there was no need to whitewash things. I remember having a sensitive conversation with Ryan, my 11-year-old son, and afterward, he said that he could have had the conversation with his dad if he was still alive. I scoffed and told him to get real. Anyone who knew my ex-husband would know the conversation I'd just had with my son would not, in any way, go over with my ex-husband – even on his most understanding day. Ryan laughed and said, he agreed. I asked him to tell me about some other things he would share with his dad, and he rattled off several. I supported him and encouraged him with each story as we both took turns giving the response we imagined his dad would give.

As I recall my romance and courtship, our marriage, the initial contention, divorce, and ultimately dynamic co-parenting, I receive all those lessons in the highest gratitude. I appreciate having the opportunity to use the disruption of divorce as an opportunity to connect with my true self and lead my family from a space of power. I am also grateful my experiences and testimony enable and beckon other women to face their pain and resentment, to overcome and heal, and to live their life from a space of co-creator standing in their power, knowing, "It's All Me."

Sources

Afua, Q, (2000). *Sacred Woman: A Guide to Healing the Feminine Body, Mind and Spirit*. New York, NY: One World Ballentine Books.

Angelou, M. (2013). Just Do Right. Retrieved from https://www.youtube.com/watch?v=bxrV2J_OjGo

Chopra, D. (1994). *The Seven Spiritual Laws of Success: A Practical Guide to the Fulfillment of Your Dreams*. San Rafael, CA: Amber-Allen Publishing.

Cooper-Sykes, S. (2016). The Confidence Class – I Believe Bootcamp Intro Retrieved from

https://www.facebook.com/watch/live/?v=10153920360996381&ref=watch_permalink

Degruy, J. (2016, July 30). What is Post Traumatic Slave Syndrome/ and the Effects Retrieved from https://www.youtube.com/watch?v=zHu6rKX4gRc

Dispenza, J. (2012). *Breaking the Habit of Being Yourself: How to Lose Your Mind and Create a New One*. Carlsbad, CA: Hay House.

Gandy, D. J. (1997). *Sacred Pampering Principles: An African-American Woman's Guide to Self-Care and Inner Renewal*. New York, NY: HarperCollins Publishing.

Goodreads. (2001, July 23). Steve Maraboli/*Quotes/ Quotable Quote*. Retrieved from https://www.goodreads.com/quotes/318941-the-truth-is-unless-you-let-go-unless-you-forgive

Hicks, A. (2019, July 22). One of THE BEST Relationship Advice (Esther Hicks Law of Attraction), Creator Within You. Retrieved from https://www.youtube.com/watch?v= XyC0S5ZIb60

Lakhiani, V. (2016) *Code of the Extraordinary Mind: 10 Unceonvential Laws to Redefine Your Life and Succeed on Your Own Terms.* New York, NY: Simon & Schuster Publishing.

McGraw, P. (2005, July 13). Advice for Parents Who are Divorcing. Retrieved from https://www.drphil.com/advice/advice-for-parents-who-are-divorcing/

Murakami, H (2006). *Kafka on the Shore.* New York, NY: Vintage Books.

OWN. (2015, August 22). *How Evelyn Learned She Was Worthy of Love and Respect/Livin' Lozada/Oprah Winfrey Network.* Retrievedfrom https://www.youtube.com/watch?v=PxKZ40cj-gw

OWN. (2018, March 6). Oprah explores "life-changing question" in treating childhood trauma. Retrieved from https://www.youtube.com/watch?v=gqu54ZlhINc

Shinn, F. S. (1925). *The Game of Life and How to Play It: The Complete Original Edition.* New York, NY: St. Martins Essentials.

Swindoll, C. (1988). *Growing Wise in Family Life.* Minneapolis, MN: Augsburg, Fortress.

Tolle, E. (2005). *A New Earth: Awakening to Your Life's Purpose.* New York, NY: Dutton/Penguin Group.

Tolle, E. (Unknown). Awakening to Your Life's Purpose. Retrieved from http://www.eckharttolletv.com/article/Awakening-Your-Spiritual-Lifes-Purpose

Tony Robbins Daily (2017, August 28) Tony Robbins Motivation- How to Raise Your Standard. Retrieved from https://youtu.be/ QkYJpNvjI5I

Vanzant, I. (2012). Why You Should Put Yourself First, Oprah's Life Class. Retrieved from https://www.youtube.com/watch?v= ZhqokZF5OFU

Wachowski, L. and Wachowski, L. (Directors). (1999). *The Matrix* [Motion picture]. United States: Warner Brothers.

Acknowledgments

Thanks Mom, for everything that I am. You are my Dianne Carrol, my Michelle Obama, and my Maya Angelou! Thank you for showing me how to remain poised in trying times, always to seek information, exude grace in my spirit, and speak eloquently and confidently. Yes, thank you for making me stand in front of the church congregation at Mount Zion MBC for every Easter speech, visitor welcome, and Sunday radio broadcast announcement. As a mom, I know it wasn't easy raising me all alone on Detroit's east side, but you did it, and you made it look easy!

My bonus Dad, Henry Eddie Hooker, you fell from the sky into my life, and I couldn't have dreamed up a better father. I often reference the lessons you've taught me, and I know you're always watching over me.

Aunt Eloise, our family matriarch, you have always made my world fun and a lighter place. Thank you for being our rock and for holding our family down.

Aunt Betty, I just love you and your radiance! Thank you for showing me how to remain in the moment, not to take everything so personal and how to keep moving forward. You inspire me!

Lisa Coker, you've been more than a cousin; you captured my heart the day you were born and have had it ever since. I adore you and thank God for who we are to each other!

Cassandra J. Harrison, on June 6, 1994, I knew you would be my big sister. I walked into Chrysler's Mound Road Engine Plant and

207

grabbed onto you for dear life. Your confidence and swag had me hooked instantly. Thank you for the countless conversations as we tried to figure out life's riddles. For laughing and crying with me and for teaching me more about life than I could ever figure out on my own, I love you.

Robin Martin, my Sister. You taught me how to wave the white flag and taught both of us (your brother and me) how to be family. You were my rock as I redefined my relationships after the divorce and a constant in the kid's life when everything else was in flux for them.

Eartha Kitt Johnson, thank you for sharing your wisdom with me. For being my stylist, my advisor, and my friend. You give the best advice, and I appreciate receiving wise counsel from you. I'm convinced you have wings hidden on your back.

Helaine Smith, my sister from another mister! I'm convinced if we did a family tree, we'd find a common relative somewhere. I love you so much and appreciate your friendship.

Jed Anantasomboon, you're always there for us. Thank you for being Uncle Jed to my children and a gracious brother to me!

Lance Schnell, you saw something in me when I didn't see it for myself. You celebrated my victories and helped me access my personal and powerful autonomy as a woman. You were there for my family and supported us as we experienced our most significant loss. You were more than my VP; you were, and still are, my dear friend and confidant; Thank you!

Love, love love to my dynamic Sorors of Delta Sigma Theta Sorority Inc. And a very special mention to my beautiful Sands-Tenacious 10: Bonita, Juanita, Bridgette, My Dearest Cousin Nicole, Chandra, LaTonya, Tammi, Carla, and Tamara 007, the person that introduced me to the possibility of living in Dallas. I love you all dearly!

Kenny Hayden & Bill Thulin, my Mound Road Engine guardian angels. You taught me so much about business, leadership, loyalty, strategy, and influence. You poured into me, and I want you to know that your legacy lives on through my children and me.

My biggest cheerleader, now watching over me with my ancestors, my Grams, Mary Belle Maiden. You made me feel like there was absolutely nothing I couldn't do. Laying my head down on your lap as you rubbed my face and brushed my hair was an elixir and balm for my soul. Your presence soothed my greatest aches, and I carry you with me daily.

A big I love you and thank you to dear friends and family, Robert Terrell, Michelle and Cedric White, Jeremy Mitchell, Bernard Hughes, Cathy Smith, Dennis Hughes, Dwayne Coker, Marci Mason, Debra Green, Norma Spearman, Ontay Johnson, Pandora Britt, Rodney Henderson, Granddad Oather Henderson, my angel and kid's bonus mom, Cindy Bryant.

About The Author

Vivian Hughes is a Mindset Coach and Brand Launch Consultant who helps executives and aspiring entrepreneurs clarify goals and create holistic success strategies.

After nearly two decades working in management for multibillion-dollar corporations and commanding 6 figure salaries in her early 20's, Vivian has learned success and perpetual goal-slaying does not always drive fulfillment!

Vivian studies human behavior patterns and triggers which allows her to help you clarify your true goals and stick to the daily small decisions that align with you achieving them.

A Detroit native who currently resides in Dallas, Texas, Vivian is a single mom of 3, she understands the importance of balance and carves out time for golf, yoga and walks in the sun regularly. Vivian is a member of Delta Sigma Theta Sorority Inc., holds a BA in business, Texas real estate license, a therapy certification, is an advanced trained PSYCH-K ® Facilitator, corporate consultant and life coach.

Vivian is available for speaking events, as well as, group, private and corporate consultation.

Vivian Hughes
PO Box 793411, Dallas, TX 75379
www.vivhughes.com

vivian@vivhughes.com

Follow On:
Facebook   : @vivianhugheselevate
Twitter   : @vivhughes606
Instagram   : @vivhughes
LinkedIn   : Vivian Hughes

www.ingramcontent.com/pod-product-compliance
Lightning Source LLC
LaVergne TN
LVHW052022080426
835513LV00018B/2115